Prai

'*Everyman's War* sensitizes us to the importance of national security and its various facets. It lends a balanced and definite view of India's inclination towards reacting 'soft' to aggression and war. Raman sets the standards high with his riveting essays. A book that challenges a reader's thought-process about war, its causes, and its consequences.'

N.R. Narayana Murthy
Executive Chairman
Infosys

'Raghu Raman's book *Everyman's War* lucidly captures the underlying issues that impact internal security and reflects his deep domain knowledge and expertise that spans across decades spent in the India Defence Services, Corporate India, and as a senior officer in the Government. His knowledge and experience equips him to take the reader right up close to short term threats and issues, and then pulls back for a long term perspective on the root causes of possible instability in the country. His ability to identify the diverse threats that we face as a nation and draw parallels from global strategies makes for compelling reading both for the chance reader and those who have been long steeped in the system. The rules of the game of internal security are continuously changing and our response must build on what history teaches us. We must also take into account the complexity of our vast geography, economic disparity, aspirations of an emerging young demography and the swift technological changes that impact each of these vectors. Raghu doesn't just identify factors that contribute to insurgency and its growth but also suggests proportionate and appropriate ways and means of addressing them. This book is compulsory reading for all those who are concerned in one way or other with India's internal security issues, as it will lead to more informed debate and decision-making on one of the most serious threats facing the country today.'

T.K.A Nair
Advisor to Prime Minister and former
Principal Secretary to Prime Minister

'Raghu Raman has done pioneering work on thinking about a security framework. This volume provides a great distillation of his thoughts. You may not agree with everything, but his reflections will incite, provoke, and deepen the debate over the relationship between security and democracy.'

Pratap Bhanu Mehta
President and Chief Executive
Centre for Policy Research

'I have avidly read Raghu's articles when they appeared in *Mint* and they were intellectually stimulating and provided a wealth of information and gave a new perspective of looking at issues. The article on Somalia and the facts of violence in USA and UK were eye-openers. I missed some of the articles and am therefore very happy that he has put them all together in a book. Easy to read and extremely illuminating, Raghu is one of the most widely read and astute commentators on internal security in India today.

It gives me great pleasure to strongly recommend this book to practitioners, academics, and the layman who will all come away greatly enriched. I am glad to have had once again the opportunity to go through this wonderful collection of articles and realize how good they read even years after they were written.'

Gopal K Pillai IAS (Retd)
Former Union Home Secretary
Government of India

'Over 25 years, Raghu Raman has zoomed in and then zoomed out, first to get a deeply personal understanding of terrorism and wars, and their impact on societies, and then to take that depth of knowledge to provide an intensely intelligent and cogent analysis of what national security, in all its ramifications, truly means to a country and its citizens. Raghu's true skill lies in taking a topic, which is often dealt with in the rarified world of think-tank experts encircled by jargon and hyperbole, or hyped incessantly on India's shrill television talk shows by politicians of all hues, and making it not just accessible but relevant to India's myriad people and their everyday lives. In three years of lucid writing for *Mint*, Raghu Raman has made a powerful case for a rethinking of India's response to internal and external threats. This compilation is essential reading to a full understanding of India's modern-day psyche, with all its strengths and flaws.'

Raju Narisetti
Founding Editor, Mint
Senior Vice President,
Deputy Head of Global Strategy, News Corp

'*Everyman's War* is an impressive compilation of short essays that highlights and brings to focus some of the most important national security issues, that have far reaching ramifications. These have for, far too long remained confined to the rarefied environs of arm-chair strategists and think tanks. Security of our country is a national endeavor and not merely the responsibility of the Armed Forces. The need of the hour is to bring in awareness and sensitize our citizens of national security issues so that these can be more meaningfully debated and understood. Raghu's book lucidly and vividly brings these issues to the fore to all—be it decision makers in the government, business, strategists, students, or the citizens. Raghu seamlessly straddles a vast canvas of security geopolitics, economics and psychology, with ease. What's more, he brings in the role of Armed Forces in the defence of the country to every-ones door step. An excellent book for those who wish to understand strategy, conflict, and terrorism that shapes our everyday lives.'

Lt Gen. K. Surendra Nath
PVSM, AVSM, VSM
Army Commander, Army Training Command

'This deftly written, highly readable book of short essays has an important message: security is full of moral ambiguity and beware of the person who claims 'moral clarity'. This is not a popular idea with hawks or those who see the world in black and white, but it is consistent with the plural, soft power of India—a country that has always been a weak state and a strong society, and whose rise is not a threat to the world, unlike China.'

Gurcharan Das
Author, Commentator, Public Intellectual

'Raghu Raman has produced a very good book from his lucid articles in *Mint* on a subject that cannot be ignored by any citizen of India. In one of his articles points to the continuing deterioration in the country's institutions and of citizens' respect for them. Raghu says the Armed Forces is the one institution all citizens respect most of all. Since he wrote those lines, leaders of the Armed Forces have been embroiled in several controversies, causing citizens to become dismayed even about the Armed Forces. He talks of the need to rebuild trust in institutions, and the need for institutionalized capabilities for collaboration amongst existing institutions. Having pointed to a widespread institutional problem in India today Raghu then focusses on agendas for reforms related to internal security. His book is a valuable compilation of ideas for solutions to the organizational crisis that is undermining the State's ability to provide security to its citizens, which citizens must become engaged with.'

Arun Maira
Member, Planning Commission of India and former
Chairman, Boston Consulting Group, India

'In this series of articles, Raghu Raman displays a deep knowledge and insight into the many complex factors that impact security issues in India. I have been an avid reader of his articles over the years and have always been impressed with his deep understanding of the complex socio-economic and geopolitical realities that are so important for appreciating this extremely nuanced subject. He has raised some red flags about the very real and interconnected challenges the country faces.

It behooves us to heed his warning call, as well as pay attention to the rather radical solutions he proposes, to keep India secure, to continue our growth trajectory and to safeguard our way of life for future generations.'

Anand Mahindra
Chairman
Mahindra & Mahindra

EVERYMAN'S WAR

EVERYMAN'S WAR

STRATEGY, SECURITY AND TERRORISM IN INDIA

R A G H U   R A M A N

RANDOM HOUSE INDIA

Published by Random House India in 2013

1

Copyright © HT Media Limited 2013

Random House Publishers India Private Limited
Windsor IT Park, 7th Floor, Tower-B
A-1, Sector-125, Noida-201301 (UP)

Random House Group Limited
20 Vauxhall Bridge Road
London SW1V 2SA
United Kingdom

ISBN 978 81 8400 426 7

This book is a compilation of the articles that have been published in MINT and the views of the author are personal.

Typeset in Goudy Old Style by Saanvi Graphics, Noida

Printed and bound in India by Replika Press Private Limited

To the courage of men who died in the line of duty
To the mettle of their families—who have to continue
battling life without them

And to my parents and my children

Contents

Lessons Learned From Armed Forces

Understanding National Security and Our Role in Safeguarding Our Own Environments

Foreword

I did not have the benefit, as some others had, of reading the author's regular column 'Cross Hairs' in *Mint*. Having gone through the various chapters of the book, *Everyman's War*—a compilation of the articles previously carried by *Mint*—I must admit that I missed something. The author with his abiding interest and knowledge in strategic and security matters, has come up with some useful insights into current security scenarios

A brief foreword is hardly the place to comment on the contents, but having spent a lifetime in the area of security, and also having been involved in some of the events that Mr Raghu Raman has chosen to comment upon in his articles, I can confidently assert that his pieces reflect both study and analysis, avoiding usual clichés and generalizations.

The true merit of the compilation to my mind lies in the fact that it sets ordinary individuals thinking about the complexity of security and strategic issues in today's world, especially in a country as vast as India. It is often said that consciousness of ignorance is the beginning of wisdom, and if Mr Raghu Raman makes people think, where previously they had chosen to remain ignorant, then he has done a great service to the nation.

I found his remark that 9/11 was 'a great return on investment' (for the terrorists responsible for the September 11, 2001 attacks) most thought-provoking, as it is true that this one single event has virtually changed the way the world functions. Likewise, this compilation of articles would be 'a great return on investment,' if people are able to better understand the various nuances of security, the connect between security policy and practice, and especially the citizenry's responsibilities, in such situations, and how they are all intertwined with the future of a nation. It drives home the point that security is everyone's concern, and that while those responsible for security can be blamed for lapses and mistakes, the citizenry cannot absolve themselves of their responsibilities.

There are one or two other aspects that I would like to draw attention to. One, the remark that despite the seeming sense of permanence, most terrorist movements come to an end, and that the end of one phase of terrorism is also the start of another. The other is the limitations of intelligence analysis, and I would supplement what the author says by mentioning that good intelligence analysis involves 'seeing with the mind's eye.' This is seldom understood, and even less appreciated. As the author himself points out, like in any other field, some are gifted and some are average in this respect.

The compilation is an easy read, and the author displays considerable prescience in the way he has analysed certain situations. It is a must read, not only for those in the business of security, but also for those who comment on security, including those in academia and in the media.

His Excellency M.K. Narayanan
Governor of West Bengal
Former National Security Advisor

Introduction

It was a bitterly cold January morning in 1988 when, as a newly minted Second Lieutenant, I was travelling on a bus to join my battalion in the small town of Sangrur in Punjab, the northern border state of India. While terrorism was on its last legs in the state, it was still very much a threat and, as the bus journeyed through the hinterland, I realized that travelling in uniform may not have been such a good idea as it made me conspicuous.

My family had no army background, and I remember many relatives and friends being concerned that I was being posted to what was then a hotbed of militancy. Instances of Khalistani separatists[1] dragging out non-Sikhs from buses and trains and shooting them were still in recent memory and at that time the army was engaged in the final stages of Operation Rakshak[2] in various parts of Punjab.

However, after a nervous 10-hour journey, I reached my unit safely. Over the next six months, I realized that while terrorism was indeed a real problem, the situation wasn't as bad as it seemed from Delhi. Young women decked out in bridal finery returning from late-night ceremonies were a common

---

[1] The Khalistani movement was an attempt by separatists in Punjab to create an enclave independent from India in the late seventies and eighties. At its zenith, the movement had become very violent and in many ways contributed to one of the worst massacres of post-independent India.

[2] Operation Rakshak, was the code name for assistance being provided to the civil administration by the Indian Army in Punjab during the late eighties and early nineties.

sight and, apart from the presence of an inordinate number of uniformed personnel (or perhaps because of it), the situation was peaceful. Over the next few months, I made friends with many locals and soon was granted my first leave after being commissioned. I told my local friends that I was going home to Delhi and was amused when they remarked that the national capital was an unsafe place, with bombs going off in buses and public places. It then struck me that insecurity, or the perception of it, depended on one's perspective more than the ground reality.

In hindsight, that realization was prescient because over the last three decades, terrorism has matured as a psychological instrument of war whose main objective is terrorizing the mind of survivors rather than notching up a tally of absolute deaths.

My journey in the field of security started in Punjab, where the threat was from armed and vicious separatists who, for all their ideological charade, were mostly just thugs leveraging the power of violence.

Next, I served in the Siachen glacier where the defence forces face a hostile enemy and the rules of engagement are nothing short of an all-out war. Where young men battle the weather as much as the adversary and come back aged several years more than the time they actually spent in sub-human conditions. In the early nineties, Siachen was perhaps the first conflict zone where many young officers, cut their teeth in full-blown operations with the entire complement of troops and equipment facing another professional army. It was also one of the first occasions in which several young officers carried the burden of their mistakes being sent home in body bags.

My third stint in operations took me as a UN peacekeeper to Africa, where the rules of engagement changed again; the job required restraint and not force. The fact that restraint required as much nerve as combat was a startling realization!

Also while protecting the nation from external aggression was a strong driver to motivate troops when deployed within the country, motivating our troops fighting for another nation, under the UN flag required a different approach altogether, especially as many of our soldiers rightfully wondered just why they were risking their lives for another country.

This tour taught me the importance of discovering new rallying points that centred on the ethos of the unit and a competitive spirit in an international arena. It was also a great opportunity to learn from other armies of the world and get a sense of our own strengths and weaknesses.

After I left the army, I spent a decade as a civilian closely involved in the domain of security and defence where I had the opportunity to realize that most civilians look at security from a very different perspective. To them, the economy comes first and security is an irritant. At times, I felt society had forgotten that security is the fundamental layer of Maslov's hierarchy of human needs. And that all elements of business, geopolitics, strategy, statecraft, and warfare have the same fundamental element at their core—more contenders vying for reducing resources. And, therefore, the successful principles of warfare could provide proven insights for virtually every kind of business or geopolitical situation.

9/11 became a game changer for the current generation and the Al Qaeda and its founders, including Osama bin Laden, became household names. While India had faced terrorism for decades and even resolved some militant movements successfully, urban India seemed to have filed away terrorism as something that happened in Kashmir or the North-east and made spectacular but sporadic appearances in the metros.

The 26/11 attacks changed all that. That day in 2008, India watched 10 men wreak unprecedented havoc in Mumbai on live TV. Suddenly, terrorism came closer and there was, understandably, much greater interest on the subject. But, strangely, we faced a paradox. For a nation that has fought major wars and is embroiled in scores of skirmishes and insurgencies on a continuous basis, most Indians know surprisingly little about defence and national security. Unlike many other nations, India has been fortunate in that it has never really faced an existential threat in living memory. And while that is a good history to have, the theatres and paradigms of modern war are changing dramatically.

War has never been about killing soldiers or civilians although it may appear to be so. This myth, propagated by movies and books, masks the reality that war is an extension of policy by other means. All warfare's essential objective is to retard the adversary's economic and geopolitical progress and advance one's own interests.

So a country might 'win' a war, battle or an engagement, but if the cost of that victory is relatively more than what the enemy had to expend, it amounts to a defeat. For instance, the Al Qaeda might have been defeated in terms of number of fighters or liquidation of their high command, but it cost the world several trillion dollars and changed our way of life forever.

A degree of ignorance might have worked until the end of the Cold War, when battles were fought by troops or by proxy, but in current times, every civilian is a stakeholder in war, national and even personal security. So awareness about matters of national security assumes greater importance. It was with this objective that I started writing the column 'Cross Hairs' in *Mint* which is in its third year now.

This book is a compilation of the articles that appeared in the paper and are divided into three broad themes, each one dealing with a particular aspect of national security, strategy, and warfare.

While each article deals with a singular issue, they all carry the common strain of circumstances that create security dilemmas and tradeoffs involved in solving them. For instance, the reader will perhaps be surprised to learn that Somali pirates have a lot in common with the Naxal movement in India or that the country with the highest defence budget of the world has more women being battered by their husbands and partners than rape, robbery, and accidents combined. This book will tell you that ecological disasters in the making have the potential to affect your children far more than all wars and conflicts put together. And show why each one of us pays the price for terrorism and insecurity on a daily basis. The book also attempts solutions that are practical and implementable at individual, organizational, and national levels. Most of all, it shows us that as a society and country—we are faced with dangerous situations which, whether we want it or not, will eventually embroil each one of us.

For as Leon Trotsky observed, 'You may not be interested in war; but war is interested in you.'

Terrorism and
Asymmetric Warfare

Tackling Guerrillas with Their Own Warfare Tactics

Strategy to deal with asymmetric warfare requires adoption of correspondingly wily tactics

In November, 2009, I had the opportunity to visit the Golden Temple at Amritsar for the first time. The grandeur and the serenity did not dilute the fact that this temple has the unique distinction of affecting the destiny of our nation in a manner whose aftermath is felt even a quarter century later.

Since I had gone to my unit for its silver jubilee celebrations, I was with many officers on this yatra. Because we were soldiers, there was no way we could not contemplate Operation Bluestar from a purely tactical angle. And as a natural extension, think about the origin and the challenges of dealing with extremist organizations. Almost as an answer, Tomar, one of my company commanders, recounted this story from Hindu mythology.

Bhasmasur, a demon from the netherworld, sought powers that would enable him to achieve dominance over the three worlds. His penance paid off with Shiva granting him a boon. Bhasmasur asked for the ability to destroy anyone he touched on the head. Impressed by Bhasmasur's devotion and convinced of his loyalty, Shiva acceded. No sooner had he done so, the demon wanted to test his powers on Shiva himself and the latter had to flee to save his life. Bhasmasur chased Shiva to kill him and take his wife Parvati for himself. In sheer desperation, Shiva, the feared destroyer, had to flee and seek refuge from Vishnu.

Demons who get their powers from the benign and then turn on the very people who supported or created them, are not new. The Taliban, the creation of the US and Pakistan, has done a Bhasmasur on its sponsors. The recent spate of attacks on Pakistani establishments is a clear indication of the demon crossing its threshold and going for the jugular of its creator.

While a lot of time is spent on studying the rise of terrorist organizations, it is equally instructive to analyse their demise. Most terrorist outfits lose their edge and deteriorate when their leaders can be made to stray from the core values or strategy that established them in the first place. Equally often, the larger-than-life image of an individual leader makes the organization vulnerable to a single point of failure. The Khalistan movement and, more recently, the Liberation Tigers of Tamil Eelam (LTTE) are good examples of how strong, well-supported movements can be systematically defeated and destroyed by targeting the fountainhead or the leaders, rather than just the frontline soldiers.

Let's consider the LTTE, for instance. V. Prabhakaran created the movement almost single-handedly. His leadership prowess had been equated with legends of guerilla warfare such as Ahmad Shah Masood, Che Guevara and even Osama bin Laden. His writ ran for around two decades (about 10 years more than Hitler's) and he had the charismatic ability to inspire women to join his armed cadre, a feat that few terrorist movements can boast of. He created the concept of suicide bombing as a force multiplier and a game changer. By any standard, Prabhakaran was a formidable leader and built a redoubtable organization.

Yet, during later years, the Sri Lankan forces could leverage the fact that the LTTE and Prabhakaran strayed from the core tenets of guerilla warfare. Instead of fighting a mobile war, consisting of hit-and-run tactics, the LTTE started getting attached to the comforts of static bases. From an inspirational leader who led from the front, Prabhakaran's image was transformed into an opulent, intransigent despot, who wanted

3

Eelam—or nothing. The very Tamils he was supposed to be fighting for were bearing the brunt of atrocities caused by his inflexibility. Any dissidence against his style of command was brutally purged, thus decimating his second line of leadership. This proved to be the LTTE's Waterloo when it was isolated in pockets during the endgame.

The Punjab terrorist movement was demolished very similarly. The government leveraged the fact that ideology had waned and racketeering was flourishing.

An essential lifeblood of terrorist and insurgency movements is the need for tacit or overt local support. Every atrocity committed by security forces strengthens the support base for the terrorist movement, which is why terrorists often provoke security forces into reprisals against innocent populations. Terror groups also have sophisticated spin doctors who present skewed views to garner support, influence opinion or mobilize funds.

While the security forces must tackle the frontline insurgents with force, the government needs to leverage instruments of transparency to demonstrate its own intent and methodology and expose the dark side of terrorism.

War in any form is a dirty business. The standards imposed on government forces are extraordinarily stringent compared with those they are battling—and it should rightly be so. But at the same time, the media and independent observers must wield their influence to disclose the instigators of terrorist movements through an unbiased lens.

Coming back to Shiva's predicament, Vishnu realized that tackling Bhasmasur required astuteness rather than force. He took the avatar of the beautiful Mohini and began seducing the demon, challenging him to a dance. Enraptured by Mohini's beauty and blinded by his lust, Bhasmasur started aping Mohini's moves until she placed her hand on her own head. Bhasmasur followed suit and was instantly reduced to ashes. Perhaps therein lies a lesson in dealing with terrorism.

The strategy to deal with asymmetric warfare necessitates adoption of correspondingly wily tactics. 'Hit-and-run' guerillas need to be countered by 'search-and-destroy' missions. When terrorists attack unsuspecting innocents, the establishment needs to respond with hot pursuit operations. Every attempt of the terrorists to demonstrate their capability to strike at will has to be replied to with an equally befitting response right up to their leadership and sponsors.

Fighting the guerillas' battle on their terms is a prolonged and a debilitating exercise, but if the establishment could leverage its capability to wean away their support bases, incapacitate their leadership capability, and force them to dance to a different tune, the demons' powers could well prove to be their downfall.

— ◆ —

The New Frontier of
Terror—Cyberspace

It is past time for India to develop a concentrated
doctrine on cyber-defence and a strategic plan that
dovetails the security of public and private networks

In December, 2009, I had the opportunity to attend a major
annual conference of information security officers from different industries in India. I have been attending such events
over the last five years and it is fascinating how the threat
scenarios discussed in these forums have changed during that
time—and frighteningly so. Until a few years ago, the biggest
threats hinged around wannabe hackers, nerdy kids and, to
some extent, practitioners of corporate espionage. We gener-
ally talked about how intellectual property rights could be
stolen or mails hacked. On more private levels, how criminals
ranging from perverts scouting their victims (usually children)
to burglars 'casing the joints' could use the Internet to solicit
or identify potential targets. But in the last few years, those
scenarios have paled in comparison to what the state, corporates, and private citizens could be subjected to. Welcome to
the age of cyber-terrorism and cyber-war.

On the afternoon of 5 November, 2009, Nidal Malik Hasan
stormed into the Fort Hood military base in Texas and shot
and killed 13 soldiers and injured 30, before he was gunned
down. Horrific though this incident was, it was by no means a
new one, except for some startling facts. Firstly, Nidal Hasan
was a serving US Marine major and posted to the base as a
psychiatrist; so not only was he was one of the 'good guys',
he was also an educated and trained government soldier.
Secondly, investigations of his emails and browsing patterns
had revealed that he was probably influenced and indoctrinated by radical fundamentalists who leveraged his Palestin-

ian descent and personal disapproval of the US invasion of Afghanistan and Iraq to motivate him to become a terrorist, using the Internet.

While this may have been one of the more dramatic instances of proliferation of fundamentalism through the Internet, it is a no-brainer that radical elements will resort to this ubiquitous channel to propagate their cause. The Internet is free, unfettered, incredibly difficult to monitor, and a truly global resource. In many ways, this strategy creates what in military parlance is called a 'turning move', because instead of attacking the strong part of the defences, the enemy turns away from them and hits from a totally different dimension, thus making barricades ineffectual.

Extrapolate this into the following actual scenarios. Radicals are casting their recruitment drive by creating underground websites preaching their cause and the alleged atrocities of the establishment. Impassioned rantings, first-person accounts of unjust persecution and doctored videos of atrocities are used to inflame and incite potential recruits. Those who visit such sites regularly, or profess sympathy, are shortlisted and 'handlers' are assigned to them. These handlers initiate personal contact through emails or chats and slowly but steadily recruit candidates into the fold, who are then subjected to brainwashing, cajoling, and finally, to direct action. This could be in the form of bombing, sabotage, espionage, or assistance to other radical members. Or, as in the case of Nidal Hasan, using the very training that he had been given and the access he was entrusted with, to kill his fellow soldiers.

In August, 2008, Russia attacked Georgia over the disputed territory of South Ossetia. This border dispute was also a harbinger of a new weapon system. While the Russian forces were mounting their operations, they were assisted by a large number of pro-Russian individuals. Websites cropped up in support of a cyber-operation, 'StopGeorgia'. Essentially, these sites had software downloads and instructions on how to use them. Any pro-Russian individual could simply enter the address of a Georgian website and block it out. As armed hostilities intensified, these denial-of-service attacks became overwhelming and effectively blocked out Georgia's capability to give out their side of the story, ensuring Russia's domination of public opinion—an essential part of any war. The interesting aspect is that Russia's conventional forces were far superior to anything that Georgia could have confronted them with. Yet, the usage of the Internet as a weapon of war was proof of the Internet's power as a force multiplier.

And here is a third scenario. The Indian information technology and telecommunications networks are expanding rapidly. Both in the private and public sector. E-governance programmes, communication grids and the explosion of cellular and financial services need millions of devices such as routers, switches, automated teller machines, and point-of-sale units. All organizations, especially the public sector, are understandably cost-conscious and look at the most economically efficient set of products while awarding such turnkey projects. Turns out that devices made in China or the Far Eastern countries win hands down on price.

Consider yourself in the shoes of the Chinese generals. Here is an opportunity to seed the entire Indian electronic, telecommunications and Internet grid with devices made by state funded and run companies—devices that are essentially black boxes to Indian buyers. Devices that can have Trojans coded into them so that they could be controlled or shut down at will by a secret command. So, if all they have to do is to make sure that their devices are the lowest in price, which they can by spending a few hundred crore rupees, wouldn't that be a brilliant return of investment?

It is past time for India to develop a concentrated doctrine on cyber-defence and a strategic plan that dovetails the security of public and private networks. Because the ubiquitous and federated nature of the Internet makes it impossible to be state guarded, this has to be a collaborative initiative between the state, private sector, and individual citizens.

The Limitations of Intelligence Analysis

The fact that the Googles, the iPhones, and the Dells of the world have come and displaced market leaders in an environment where the facts were apparently for all to see and use, proves that developing intelligence is not as easy as just having all the information

As a small boy growing up in Delhi, I remember sleeping out on the terrace during summers. During those nights, my father would often point out the constellations and teach me how to identify them. The Orion, Big Dipper, Cassiopeia and the Indian variants such as the Saptarishi. As a kid, it seemed to me that if I stared at the sky long enough, I could pretty much imagine any shape I wanted to. The business of intelligence is a bit like that. If you stare long enough at events that have passed, you could always come up with the question—why didn't we see that happening? But there are some very good reasons why we don't see obvious events coming.

The Pearl Harbor, the Bay of Pigs, fall of the Berlin Wall, the Yom Kippur war, 9/11 or the Mumbai terror attacks—the list goes on. These seem to have been totally predictable events (world changing events at that)—after the fact—and yet experienced analysts, political observers, intelligence agencies, and even powerful governments seem to have been completely blindsided by them. Businesses are no better, by the way. Established business leaders routinely fail to spot or leverage disruptive technologies, paradigm shifts, or changing customer preferences. The fact that the Googles, the iPhones, and the Dells of the world have come and displaced market leaders in an environment where the facts were apparently for all to see and use, proves that developing intelligence is not as easy as just having all the information.

One of my favourite examples is an incident of failure of intelligence taught in military curriculums. The story goes something like this. In 1967, Israel won the six-day war against half-a-dozen countries. This victory came with the price of humiliated and belligerent enemies and a very volatile neighbourhood. While there were sporadic periods of peace, there was underlying tension, with Egypt vowing revenge and retribution. From 1972, the then president Anwar Sadat began earnestly preparing Egypt's armed forces. Acquisition of weapons, step-up of training and reconnaissance, buttressing of defences and repositioning of artillery were all signs that something major was afoot.

Towards the end of September and through the first week of October 1973, the signs of war became dramatically obvious. Russian advisers in Egypt were moving out their families and Golda Meir, the Israeli prime minister, received a warning about the impending attack directly from King Hussein of Jordan. Mossad chief Zvi Zamir continued to hold the view that war was not an Arab option. He was wrong. Syria and Egypt attacked Israel on 6 October, 1973 in what was the bloodiest war that Israel had ever fought.

Why did intelligence fail in this instance? Or as in the case of several other instances in world history. It is because intelligence doesn't fail. Intelligence is not a project—which can fail or succeed. It's a process that has elements of planning and execution and so for 'intelligence' to succeed, it needs to be acted upon successfully. So why don't decision makers act on intelligence? That is because of two factors.

One, specific intelligence is very hard to come by in real time. Yes, the dots do exist, and while they are easy to connect post facto, it is exceptionally difficult to do that in real time.

Even extremely predictable cyclical events such as economic volatility leave experts flummoxed.

To see why this happens, let us go back to Israel in 1970. At that point in Egypt, Sadat became president after Gamal Abdel Nasser had died. For over three years, there was intense pressure on him to avenge the defeat of the six-day war. From the time he took over, Sadat was vociferous in his articulation of Egypt's intention to retaliate. Egypt mobilized its army over a dozen times in 1973—and nothing happened. Trusted sources gave warnings of attacks and no attacks took place. Such false positives take a heavy toll on security apparatuses. For instance, each time a city goes on alert, it causes incredible damage and trauma. Airlines and passengers lose millions every year because of airport alerts, millions of man-hours are lost because of security checks on roads, airports, hotels, hospitals, and malls. The very act of acting on intelligence can make a society behave as if under a siege. Also, there is intense pressure on the intelligence advisers—not to be wrong.

And this leads to a second phenomenon called 'committed credibility.' Intelligence analysts are like doctors. They read signs, use their tools, training, and experiential knowledge to diagnose situations. Like in any other field, some are gifted and some are average. Their diagnosis is used by decision makers to decide on courses of action. But like complex diseases, no diagnosis can be truly conclusive. There are always elements missing, and each new piece of information has the potential to transform the diagnosis, sometimes drastically.

When I was in my early twenties, I was once again staring at the skies in Dehradun, this time under the watchful gaze of my instructors in the Indian Military Academy. They were teaching me the constellations all over again, but now, it was with a very specific purpose—to locate the North Star and get directions. And again, intelligence is a bit like that. It gives us directions and guidance, but there is no getting away from the fact that like any diagnosis, there will be failures. Which is why as a society and a nation, our ability to respond must be swift and decisive because the hope of prevention cannot be a strategy.

The Endgame of Terror

There are at least six ways to finish terrorist groups.
A one-size-fits-all approach seldom delivers results

Despite their seeming sense of permanence, most terrorist movements come to an end. Being at the epicentre of some of the longest such movements, this may not be apparent to most Indians. The bad news is that the end of terrorism may not necessarily mean the beginning of peace. As Audrey Cronin of Oxford University observes, states ought to study the final phases of terrorist movements with the same fervour as their origins, because that is where the key to ending them lies ('How Terrorism Ends: Understanding the Decline and Demise of Terrorist Campaigns'). From a strategic point of view, terrorism ends in six distinct ways that are unique to the movement, its origins, genre and several other parameters. One approach to ending terror clearly does not fit all circumstances.

Decapitation, or specifically targeting the senior leadership of the terrorist movement, is the first of these strategies. Israel and the US use this approach extensively, but with mixed dividends. Leadership is a critically scarce resource for terrorists as it takes years to cultivate the unique blend of ruthlessness, charisma, stamina, and organizing capabilities needed to lead terror groups. States have two options in taking out leaders: They could either capture and imprison them, or aim to liquidate them. Of course, the viability of either option is also a primary deciding factor, but both of them have different strategic implications.

Attacking the leadership with the intent to kill in some sense recognizes them as combatants, thus legitimizing their claims of fighting a 'war' against the state. On the other hand, by capturing and imprisoning them, the state elevates its moral ground and reduces the captured leader to a common criminal. Of course, the latter option is far more difficult for a variety of reasons, least of which is the ability to capture leaders and the high casualty rates in such operations. In addition, the state runs the risk of having to release them later as a result of sloppy judicial processes or other terrorist activities such as the IC 814 highjack in 1999, which was mounted specifically to secure the release of three terrorists, each of whom promptly went back to terrorism with a vengeance (Masood Azhar was involved in the Indian Parliament attack, Ahmed Omar Saeed Sheikh killed The Wall Street Journal reporter Daniel Pearl, and Mushtaq Zargar has been training militants in Pakistan-occupied Kashmir since his escape).

Decapitation as an instrument to battle terror, however, works best when the leadership of the organization is autocratic and central, and there is no credible second line (such as in the case of V. Prabhakaran of the Liberation Tigers of Tamil Eelam). However, the state needs to be cognizant that liquidating leaders may instantly idolize them as martyrs, such as Che Guevara, and even spawn new factions such as Hamas that are far more radical than the original leaders.

The second option is a negotiated end to terrorism. This intuitively appears to be the sane and mature solution, but it is ironically far more complex. From the state's perspective, it's a devil's alternative. If the state is seen to be negotiating with terrorists, then they open a Pandora's box of factions wanting to 'bomb their way' to the negotiating table. Also, many of the demands that terrorists place, such as secession or blanket amnesty for all past acts, are simply impossible for the state to accede to. Finally, terrorist groups are notorious for using the negotiating period for rearmament and recouping, and then reneging on the process on some frivolous excuse.

From the terrorist's perspective, negotiating with the state is fraught with the danger of creating factions between the radical and moderate elements of the terror movement. Also, while the state wants to end terrorism, many terrorists want to keep it alive because they draw their raison d'être from terrorism. Terrorists, unlike insurgents, do not capture and hold territory; and so terrorist attacks are a necessity for their significance to be kept alive.

Finally, to commence negotiation, it is critical that both the state and the terrorists are convinced of a deadlock. If either side believes it is dominant, then there is no reason for it to negotiate. On the flip side, if the state agrees to negotiate without at least a precondition, such as a stop on all further attacks, it signals its acknowledgement of an impasse. It is perhaps for this reason that historically, less than 20 percent of terrorist groups have ever had a negotiated end. Northern Ireland and, closer home, the Bodo movement are examples. However, there are certain conditions under which negotiation has a good chance of success. Unless these are in place, it is pointless even attempting to negotiate.

Implosion, or self-destruction, is the third reason why a terrorist movement can eventually end. This could be because the movement loses momentum, or attrition by the state proves to be overwhelming for it to sustain. Sometimes it is because terrorist leaders are not able to control or motivate cadres, or pass their commitment and knowledge to the next generation. Infighting or internal power struggles is another reason why movements can implode. Indiscriminate targeting, especially of women and children, marginalizes the terrorists—the very population whose cause they claim to propound begins to cooperate with the state out of sheer disgust and fatigue. The Khalistani separatist movement is a prime example of such an end.

— ◈ —

The Endgame of Terror–II

Terrorism is a battle for perception. The ways in which it ends hold lessons for all, not just the state and its forces

The previous chapter discussed three of the six ways in which terror movements come to an end. To continue with the discussion, overwhelming and repressive campaigns against terrorists is the fourth and perhaps the most common approach that states resort to. This is a natural response that history is replete with—colonial powers such as the British in India used this very approach to try and suppress what they perceived to be secessionist terrorism.

In a way, the state has to demonstrate an immediate and rapid response to terror movements—more, to assuage its broader set of stakeholders, than what the immediate problem requires. Its motive is clear: The need to be seen as 'doing something' is a reinforcement that the state is in control. And this show of force is critical. Terrorists aim to attack the morale of the public and suggest that they, and not the state, are in control. Armed troops rushing to the affected region, area dominance through intensive patrolling, cordon and search operations, and other state measures are designed to replace terror with a sense of order and steadfastness.

The Peruvian government's response to the Maoist Shining Path movement, Russia's response to the Chechen rebels and the Turkish response to the Kurds fall in this category. Such repression is accompanied by high collateral damage, with innocent people being displaced, incarcerated, or killed. By definition, a heavy hand and subtle nuances don't go together, thus leading to extrajudicial atrocities and abuses, which in turn alienate state forces and offer recruitment opportunities to the terrorists. Fortunately, history shows that security forces soon learn from their mistakes and initiate specific targeting, efforts to win over the hearts and minds of the people, and focus on intelligence-based operations. However, history also shows us that the state's slow recognition of the magnitude of the problem and its lack of urgency or intelligence-based operations make the situation a lot worse before it can become better.

The repressive approach is characterized by high casualties, displacements, abuse, and a deep sense of polarization which ultimately come back to haunt the state in other forms. Democracies are particularly at a disadvantage in this approach because its implementation requires the suspension of some elements of a democratic framework.

The fifth situation is where the terrorist group reorients itself to either an upstream model, graduating to a full-blown insurgency or separatist movement (such as the Liberation Tigers of Tamil Eelam, or LTTE) or slips downstream into criminal activities, like the Khalistanis. Terrorist movements straddle a thin line between guerrilla warfare and criminality. The ideological leadership of such movements tries to leverage a sense of purpose and values as the central themes, but militant wings gravitate towards criminal activities such as kidnapping, extortion, drug dealing, smuggling, and theft. Of course, while almost all terrorist movements indulge in both these activities, the key is to discern where their bias is. This is usually decided by the centrality and legitimacy of the cause espoused by the movement and the diaspora that can support it. If a large part of the movement's funding comes from legitimate sympathizers who identify with its cause, or from foreign states that want to foment trouble, then the movement is more likely to escalate into an insurgency. If, on the other hand, the terrorist organization depends on extortion and forced 'donations', then it quickly degenerates into common criminality, loses its popular base, and becomes less of a threat to the state.

The last scenario in which terrorism ends is when the group achieves its intention. The current world order, especially in Europe and post-colonial Asia, is a derivative of successful movements with significant terrorist incidents that have been legitimized by the victors, and history has reflected that legitimization. Ireland, the African National Congress in South Africa and, more recently, the Maoist regime in Nepal are examples where the terrorist elements have lived out their locus standi once their respective goals were achieved. Historically, such instances are rare—limited to situations where a minority ruled over an overwhelmingly dissatisfied majority. Statistically, there are more examples of terrorism achieving very limited success or completely failing the people they purported to represent, while the movement's leaders themselves benefited materially.

Audrey Cronin's assessment of terrorism's end (*How Terrorism Ends: Understanding the Decline and Demise of Terrorist Campaigns*) has lessons for India as well. We face terrorist threats from multiple movements of different genres and motivations. A fundamentalist radical group led by a charismatic leader needs a different approach than, say, a federated, foreign-aided movement such as Naxalism. We must also realize that solutions which appear ideal, such as negotiation, for instance, have their own lengthy timetables. Hence, stakeholder expectations need to be managed accordingly. And this understanding of the end of terrorism should not be limited to just the security forces and the state. Terrorism, after all, is a battle for perception. Unless all participants realize the nuances of the different endgames of terrorism, they could be learning the wrong lessons from the right battles.

— ◈ —

Citizens on the
First Line of Defence

Two years after the Mumbai attacks, Indians still need a
paradigm shift in their approach to asymmetric warfare

26 November, 2010 marked the second anniversary of the
attacks that changed the way this country thinks about terrorism. Despite India being no stranger to terror attacks, 26/11
struck deeper than any prior assault, and rallied the country
like never before. There was cold rage among the masses, and
seemingly enough realization in the establishment for it to
take major structural steps—from lobbying in global forums,
changing leadership, and commencing or strengthening strategic anti-terror initiatives. The quintessential new question is
this: Two years down the line, is India safer?

The answer is yes and, unfortunately, no.

Let me explain this paradox with an example. The US government had recognized the threat from Islamic fundamentalists
long before 9/11, and had been lobbying intensely for the
empowerment of law enforcement agencies to deal with the
peculiarities of asymmetric warfare. That didn't happen until
Al Qaeda struck on 9 September, 2001. Less than six weeks
later, the US president enacted the Patriot Act, increasing law
enforcement agencies' intelligence gathering capabilities and
jurisdiction. Anyone remotely familiar with bureaucracy will
appreciate that there was no way such a complicated Act could
have been passed in such a short time unless detailed preparation had begun several years ago.

A decade down the line, despite a couple of close calls, the
US can boast of a fairly unblemished internal security track
record, not only because it invested heavily in counter-terror
capabilities, but also because it rapidly changed environmental
elements in order to deal with the new threat.

India, too, has made substantial progress in building institutional capability to combat terror. But it needs significant work in addressing the environment in which these institutions can deliver results. And these changes have to be paradigm shifts in the way Indians realign themselves to the threat of asymmetric warfare.

The first of these shifts has to be a realization that government establishments can do only so much to combat terror. Terrorists operate and thrive within the public infrastructure that society uses. They use banks to transfer funds; airlines, road and railways to travel; cellular networks to communicate; and sleeper cells within communities to conceal themselves. In other words, they use the same infrastructure they seek to destroy. So there is no one better poised than the bankers, the telecom and airline operators, and the citizens within the community to identify the outlier behaviour that acts as early warning signals of imminent attacks. Citizens must realize that they are not just victims, but also the frontline troops in the battle against terror. And instead of expecting security forces to be omnipresent, they must facilitate the omnipresence of security.

The second shift is the recognition that asymmetric threats require a fundamental change in the way we think about our current socio-political scenario. Democracy pivots on civil liberties. But civil liberties are meaningless without civil security. Changing threat scenarios require society to re-think priorities between contradictory requirements.

Hence, an expectation that terrorists will be identified and pre-empted requires observation and analysis of information, which may be construed to be intrusive. Society must make the decision about what to give up to achieve a larger objective.

But there is a perpetual lag between realizing what needs to be done and gaining the momentum to do it. Even something as obvious as preventing smoking in public places required millions of needless deaths before activists were convinced of its merits. Similarly, while events such as 26/11 act as catalysts, public memory is short, and complacency empowers cynics and the champions of status quo. Wars, however, are won on sustained, resolute action and not on spurts of rhetoric.

The third and most important awakening is that structural improvements take radical thought. Institutions and initiatives must be nurtured and supported through this gestation period.

Terrorists use guerilla tactics, leveraging its agility. Countries, societies and their governments, on the other hand, are like supertankers at sea. They need lead time to adjust to the new course. History shows us that terrorism is eventually beaten. But the question is: What price will society pay for not changing course soon enough? The ability of the enemy to inflict immense damage with low investment is only possible because society clings to old paradigms.

After World War I, the French built the Maginot Line, a series of fortifications all along its eastern borders, and relied on the security of this static system. The German invasion forces in World War II overcame this much-vaunted defence within five days, simply by flanking it with highly mobile forces.

Similarly, countries the world over responded to the Mumbai style of attacks by building fortifications around hotels and public places at a cost of millions of dollars. Al Qaeda's latest tactic of using postal bombs—with a self-admitted investment of less than $5,000—is expected to cost society $4.5 billion in prevention. With such skewed ratios, it is clear who is winning.

And these ratios will not change unless we alter the paradigm of reacting to terrorists. There is no 'Ring of Steel' that will keep the enemy at the gates. The enemy is already inside the gates. So, we must realize that to combat an amorphous enemy, we need a ring of early warning, of intelligence—a ring that is built by the community for itself, and by itself.

Terrorism's Ultimate
Smart Bomb

The operational value of suicide attacks ensures that the
deadliest form of terrorism will increase in frequency

On 30 October, 1980, in the midst of the Iran–Iraq war, the
Iranian army was defending the key town of Khorramshahr in
southern Iran. The Iraqi forces were on the verge of making a
breakthrough. Iranian soldiers had taken heavy casualties, and
their ability to resist the advancing Iraqis was fast evaporating.
At this point, Hossein Famideh, a young Iranian, strapped
explosives to his body and ran into the leading line of Iraqi
tanks, blowing them and himself to bits.

Famideh's suicide attack halted the Iraqi advance, rallied
the Iranians, and turned the battle in their favour. Ayatollah
Khomeini declared Famideh a national hero, and a tomb was
erected in his honour outside Tehran. His death, or martyrdom—as Iranians saw it—inspired several legends and sagas
that are recounted in Iranian schools to this day.

Hossein Famideh, the world's first suicide bomber, was 13
years old when he died.

Within two years, several hundred Iranian soldiers were
copying Famideh's feat, and 'martyrdom' had become an
acknowledged Iranian weapon of war. In 1982, the Iranians
helped create one of the most feared Islamic terror groups—the
Hezbollah, or the 'Party of God,' in response to the Israeli
invasion of Lebanon. In addition to getting financial aid,
weapons, and training, the Hezbollah also learnt the force
multiplier effect of the suicide bomber.

On 11 November, 1982, 19-year-old Ahmed Qasir drove a
car filled with explosives into an Israeli barrack in the southern Lebanese city of Tyre, killing 74 and injuring scores more.

With this, Qasir became the world's first car bomber, and 11 November became known as Martyr's Day in Lebanon.

Just six months later, on 18 April, another suicide bomber struck the US embassy in Beirut, killing 60 people and gutting the building totally. Incredibly, another six months later, on 23 October, two suicide bombers struck the US and French barracks, causing the largest casualty on a single day in the history of the Marine Corps since the battle of Iwo Jima in 1945, and the largest non-nuclear explosion since World War II. These twin blasts led to the death of nearly 300 soldiers and the withdrawal of the international peacekeeping forces from Lebanon, thus establishing the strategic role of the suicide bomber in modern irregular warfare. In 2005, a study by Robert Pape of the University of Chicago chronicled a total of 462 suicide attacks between 1980 and 2004.

To appreciate the finer point of suicide attacks, it is important to distinguish this strategy from committing suicide in protest, (for example, self immolations by Tibetan nationalists protesting against the Chinese) or suicide missions where there is a strong possibility of eventual death (like the fidayeen attacks in Kashmir). The essential distinction of the suicide attack is that suicide is the centrality of the attack itself, like the 9/11 attacks on the World Trade Centre.

Interestingly, secular groups, and not Islamic fundamentalists, have been responsible for more than half of suicide attacks, with the Liberation Tigers of Tamil Eelam (LTTE)— a Marxist group— holding the top spot. Secular groups with Marxist or anti-religious beliefs (such as the PKK, a Kurdish terrorist organization) also account for more than one-third of Islamic terrorist attacks.

There are, however, some commonalities between suicide attacks across Lebanon, Chechnya, Russia, Sri Lanka, Israel,

Turkey, Afghanistan, Iraq and even India. The first is the terrorists' objective of compelling the removal of what they see as an occupation force; or, as in the case of Rajiv Gandhi's assassination, a preemptive effort to forestall such a deployment.

The second is that suicide attacks are usually carried out by 'walk-in' fanatics who are not long-time members of terror groups. In some instances, they approach the terrorist organizations just days before the attack, with the sole purpose of carrying out that one devastating act. That, coupled with the absence of an escape strategy, halves the usual planning and logistics that go into terrorist attacks, and makes the suicide attacker very difficult to profile or track.

Motivations for suicide attacks vary from seeking prestige, peer pressure, revenge, or religious ideology. Paradoxically, such attacks are seldom driven by abject poverty or ignorance.

Statistics show that most suicide attackers belong to the middle class, and are better educated than the average.

This has relevance for us, because apart from fidayeen attacks in the Kashmir valley and the 2008 Mumbai attacks (the latter can be argued to be a suicide mission rather than a suicide attack), India has been largely untouched by this genre of terrorism. But that is likely to change, as suicide attacks gain salience across the world. More worryingly, such attacks have proven to be the deadliest form of terrorism. Although they constitute fewer than 5 percent of all terrorist attacks, they cause nearly 50 percent of the fatalities—too attractive a return for terrorist organizations to ignore, and an effective rallying call for potential recruits.

And while relatively low-impact acts such as the recent blast in Varanasi jolt us out of complacency, the suicide bomber is the ultimate smart bomb—a fact that terrorists know only too well, and a tool they will resort to sooner than later.

— ◈ —

Terrorist and Social Media

The Internet is redefining terrorism: from planning to actual attacks, all can be executed from a safe distance

The irony of terrorism is that terrorists don't want to kill a lot of people. That is not their ultimate objective. Their target is the billions who get terrorized and hence the propaganda aspect of the attack is critical to terrorism.

This centrality of 'broadcasting' terror makes media exploitation a linchpin for both terror and counter-terror strategies. Unarguably, terrorism makes for a good news stories and acts of terror get top mindshare. However, proliferation of the Internet and social media is becoming the game changer in terrorism in three distinct ways.

Prior to the Internet, terrorists had to depend on conventional TV or print channels to reach their intended audience. This had some inherent difficulties. Firstly, it limited the theatre of operations to areas where the media could reach fast independently. But this meant that the security forces could also get there just as fast. Secondly, media would play the story the way they wanted it, which sometimes meant censoring the more horrific footages and also painting the terrorists in criminal brushstrokes rather than the ideological positioning terrorists craved. Another problem with the conventional media was that they could be state-controlled or at the very least influenced. In some notable cases, the media had even cooperated with the government by withholding information or feeding misinformation to confuse the terrorists.

While some terrorist organizations got around these difficulties by sending videotapes of their acts, especially kidnappings, hostage executions or pre-bombing speeches to TV channels or cultivating sympathetic channels by promising them exclusives, media control continued to be a challenge. The advent of the Internet solved the media-control problem as the terrorists could now retail direct to the audience without the interference of conventional media. The more innovative ones created different versions of the footage in multiple languages to reach wider audiences. They also leveraged the benefits of viral 'marketing' as sympathizers or voyeurs, fascinated by the macabre, would relay these footages through the Internet. And at times they hit a propaganda goldmine.

On 29 May, 2004, terrorists struck various facilities in Al Khobar region of Saudi Arabia. At Oasis 3, one of those complexes, about a dozen terrorists shot their way in and executed several non-Muslims in cold blood. These included eight Indians. The murderers stayed in the complex through the next five hours and calmly ate breakfast. But as there was no meaningful response from law enforcement agencies beyond the encirclement of the complex, most of the terrorists just slipped past the enclosure and actually managed to film the government force's helicopters that came in to liberate the complex. The Saudi government forces announced success of the operation, much of which was countered by the terrorist organization Jerusalem Squadron that claimed responsibility and released Internet clippings that showed an-hour-long movie of the terrorists' siege and subsequent escape. This film got wide propaganda and caused panic among the expatriates resulting in, among other things, driving up the oil price to $42 a barrel. All that damage with a $50 camera and the Internet.

The second role social media plays is closely linked with propaganda—recruitment. Terrorist organizations face the challenge of reaching out to potential new cadres. Before the proliferation of social media, this activity had problems of scale and was fraught with danger. Recruitment involved direct physical contact with the pool of potential recruits, effort of pre-qualification, preliminary indoctrination, and the final act of recruitment itself. This entire process could come under surveillance or even infiltration by law enforcement and undercover operatives and, therefore, had high exposure risks.

The Internet has changed that too. Now websites and chat rooms can be used to establish contact, pre-qualify, indoctrinate, and even coordinate missions. On 5 November, 2009, Nidal Hasan, a serving US Army major, used his service rifle to gun down 13 comrades in Fort Hood, Texas army base. Hasan had been indoctrinated and deeply influenced by Anwar al-Awlaki, a fundamentalist spiritual leader who motivated and guided him, helping him overcome any moral compunctions he might have had to slaughter innocent people. This activity took place over the Internet with Awlaki using his blog to broadcast his radical preaching and a series of email exchanges to push Hasan into committing this act.

The third element is the terrorist's rapid adoption of the Web technology to communicate, recce targets, collaborate, and coordinate terrorist activity from the obscurity of the Internet. There are sites with elaborate instructions on bomb making, forging identity and travel papers, weaknesses of targets, and everything else that an aspiring terrorist needs in terms of knowledge. Obtaining the tools of committing terror is as easy as obtaining music online.

The Internet gives a powerful strategic advantage to terrorists. While they can hack mails, assume false identities and aliases, wire money to fund terrorist activities, and leverage every nefarious capability of the Internet, law enforcement agencies are hamstrung by stringent privacy and data protection laws and covenants. This tilts the playing field in favour of the terrorists and weakens the fight against them.

— ◆ —

The Myth of Zero Tolerance

Acts of terrorism thrive on the same global illicit trade
networks that some of us unknowingly help sponsor

The previous chapter described how the Internet and social
media have exacerbated the effectiveness of terror. This
phenomenon is not just an extension of terrorism's physical
manifestation in another domain. Instead, it is a paradigm
shift in the way terrorists have subverted the global network
to wreak havoc.

Surprisingly, many of us participate in this network. At
times, we even facilitate the proliferation of organized crime
and terrorism. Shocked? Read on.

It is estimated that over 10 percent of all global trade is illicit.
This includes fakes of Louis Vuitton bags, Gucci shoes, Rolex
watches, famous apparel labels, as well as pirated movies,
software, and music. Most people think of this as a harmless
'no-loss' crime.

But illicit trade doesn't end there. Over 10 percent of all
medicines consumed in the world are estimated to be spurious. This figure is 25 percent in India. More than 37 percent
of auto parts sold here are counterfeit. Narcotics, weapons,
conflict diamonds, endangered wildlife, human body parts,
and sex slaves are traded illicitly all over the world. The Internet has multiplied the market reach of such goods across continents through a sophisticated supply chain that rides on legitimate business conduits.

The splicing of legitimate and illegitimate businesses
manifests itself in the laundering of billions of dollars generated
by illicit trade. This dirty money hops across countries and
accounts, and eventually funnels into legitimate businesses,
many of which operate as fronts to facilitate the laundering
process.

Illicit trade has swollen into organized crime at a global scale. Like any global trade, it has a network of intermediaries who procure the contraband from the source, and transport it through various conduits until it retails to the end customer. Coca leaves harvested in Columbia are refined in Mexico and transported to streets in the US and Europe using sophisticated delivery channels that include aircraft, high- speed boats, and even submarines. Along the way, border guards, customs, and other law enforcement entities have been incorporated into the business, so much so that even large contraband seizures hardly dent the street price. This indicates the multitude of channels through which these pass, and their tenacity.

Illegal trade has become so pervasive that their retail markets often operate in open view. Every city has its own illegal goods street, which can be found in tourist guidebooks. There are other less known but equally accessible markets—Dara Adam Khel in Pakistan manufactures thousands of weapons, from AK-47s to anti-aircraft guns. It is ironic that while the US attacked Iraq on suspicions of producing weapons of mass destruction, A.Q. Khan—the father of Pakistan's nuclear programme—was peddling blueprints and nuclear technology to Iraq, Libya, and North Korea.

This problem becomes increasingly menacing when the conduits that service illicit goods are used for more sinister cargo such as weapons, explosives, classified know-how, and physical transportation of terrorists.

A future terrorist threat scenario could leverage the illicit supply chain that stretches across continents. It could source explosives from one country, the technical expertise to manu-facture dirty nuclear devices from another, ship the bomb in one of the millions of containers that criss-cross the globe, land it in ports that check only a fraction of the cargo, and move it through the lattice of corrupt officials right to the target. This supply chain that transports thousands of smuggled goods or drugs can easily carry high explosives with impunity.

There is no such thing as mild corruption. Terrorists know this Achilles' heel in the system too well. The current scale of organized crime would have been impossible without the connivance of officials and the state machinery. In such a scenario, identifying and intercepting terror-related consignments or transactions, among other contraband, is like looking for a needle in a stack of needles.

In 2002, Chechen terrorists killed over 200 people at a Moscow theatre. A year later, they massacred over 350 people, including 186 children, at a school in Beslan. In both these instances, the heavily armed terrorists allegedly drove in minivans all the way from Chechnya, bribing their way through checkpoints. It is also estimated that a high degree of corruption among security personnel was instrumental in facilitating the bombing of the Moscow airport last month.

Closer home, in Mumbai, powerful blasts killed over 250 people and injured 1400 others in March, 2003, making it the most devastating single-day attack ever. This operation was masterminded by the Inter-Services Intelligence (ISI), using notorious gangster Dawood Ibrahim's resources to transport 3,000 kg of RDX used in the blasts, and his henchmen for executing the attacks. Over a hundred people were convicted, of which the prosecution sought death penalty for 44.

Those convicted included two landing agents, five customs officials, and two policemen. The prosecution alleged that these individuals had facilitated the landing of the explosives despite knowing the deadly nature of the consignment, in return for bribes.

Societies have to decide when enough is enough and start making paradigm shifts of their own to address this issue in a proactive, systematic, and structured manner. It is impossible to have a zero tolerance response to just terrorism in an environment that is tolerant of every other crime.

— ◆ —

Intelligence as Force Multiplier

The Battle of Britain showed intelligence could upstage numbers. That realization is important for India's forces

Intelligence, more than any other asset, can be a game changer in conflicts. An example from World War II illustrates this.

In May 1940, the British Army lay devastated at the French harbour of Dunkirk. In full retreat and with their morale low, over 330,000 troops were evacuated from the European theatre. Winston Churchill described it as a 'colossal military disaster', admitting that the army's equipment, core, and brain were in a shambles on the beaches of Dunkirk.

With the Nazi gaining complete dominance over Europe, Hitler was confident that the depleted British would have no option but to press for an armistice. But Britain continued to be defiant. After France surrendered in June, Hitler ordered preparations for a sea-borne invasion of Britain, called Operation Sea Lion.

The contours of the German invasion plan were straightforward. It envisaged an armada of barges that would transport the invasion force and land them along the eastern coast of Britain. In anticipation, the British had thrown together remnants of their army and virtually every able-bodied soul into homeland defence along the coastline and at ports.

To succeed, the Germans needed to cross the English Channel without interference from the British Navy—still a formidable force. This required the German Air Force—the Luftwaffe—to achieve air superiority during the crossing. Hermann Goering, the Luftwaffe commander, was supremely confident of his ability to provide that air cover, because Luftwaffe outnumbered the Royal Air Force (RAF) by a factor of three.

In July, the Germans attacked British shipping in the English Channel, with devastating results. RAF fighters were hopelessly outnumbered. Soon, the Luftwaffe and German U-boats had stopped almost all British traffic through the channel.

Next, the Germans began attacking coastal airfields to destroy RAF capabilities and launch pads. And despite Hitler's specific directives not to bomb London, the Luftwaffe first inadvertently and then deliberately attacked the capital, bombing it almost every day.

RAF realized its Achilles' heel was numerical inadequacy, and that it could not engage the Luftwaffe in pitched battles. Even if its pilots performed magnificently, the superior German numbers would simply decimate them in sortie after sortie.

And so, the British developed a secret weapon, the 'Dowding' system, named after air chief marshal Sir H.T.C. Dowding. This system consisted of 21 radar towers deployed along the eastern coast of Britain, and tasked to detect German air raids well before they approached the mainland. The strength, composition, and thrust lines of the raiding parties were fed through a sophisticated system of telephones and wireless to the main control room, from where operational instructions were relayed to RAF squadrons best poised to confront the Luftwaffe.

The result was that RAF fighters seemed to magically appear whenever the Luftwaffe approached strategic targets. The Dowding system also leveraged Bletchley Park—the British code-breaking organization that had deciphered the German Enigma machines and could thus provide valuable intelligence by intercepting German communication.

This integrated system of information coming in penny packets from the radars, observers, Bletchley Park, and other sightings was assembled to present a strategic picture to the British high command.

RAF decided to offset its numerical disadvantage by engaging only major German formations at tactically advantageous moments. The Dowding system allowed it to choose the killing ground and engage the Luftwaffe when it was more vulnerable—such as during the return trip, when fuel would be running low.

The radar was a relatively recent invention, and Goering didn't appreciate the potential of this paradigm-shifting technology. The uncanny ability with which RAF fighters seemed to intercept the Luftwaffe frustrated him and forced him to assign more fighter escorts to the bombers. This aggravated the situation, because the German fighters now had less room to manoeuvre.

The Battle of Britain, as this campaign came to be known, was the first time that an integrated system was used in real time to defeat a numerically stronger enemy. Faced with such strategic intelligence, Goering was unable to provide the air superiority essential for the German assault. Soon, the US and the Soviet Union joined the war against the Axis powers, forcing Hitler to abandon his invasion plans.

The Dowding system allowed the British to use strategic intelligence as a force multiplier, enabling optimum use of scarce resources. Lacking a similar framework—and, more importantly, the vision to appreciate its value—the German high command fought the battle blind and far removed from the ground reality. It eventually lost to a force that was numerically disadvantaged, but strategically insightful.

The operational situations that India faces in its internal conflicts are highly fluid and opaque. Opportunities are fleeting and their immediate exploitation is critical, especially for conventional forces that by their very design are rigid and slower in response compared with their irregular adversaries. The only way security forces can offset this disadvantage is by implementing integrated frameworks that give them visibility of weak signals at their earliest occurrence. This would allow deployment of resources with surgical precision during the early stages of planning and attack, rather than force strategists to rely only on numerical superiority in later stages or post facto.

Terrorism Thrives
in the Fault Lines

As the origins of one of the longest lasting conflicts in
human history show, an act of terror is seldom just that

On 28 June, 1914, a 19-year-old Bosnian, Gavrilo Princip,
executed a terror attack of cataclysmic proportions. The shots
he fired not only killed Archduke Franz Ferdinand, heir to the
Austro-Hungarian throne, but also caused a series of upheav-
als that redrew boundaries of European nations and toppled
four major dynasties, including the Ottoman Empire. World
War I, which claimed around 10 million lives over four-and-a-
half years and devastated large parts of the globe, started with
that single terror incident.

Yet, as Harvard professor of history Niall Ferguson points
out (in *The War of the World*), political assassinations were fairly
common in the early twentieth century. Four kings, six prime
ministers, and three presidents were among the 40 heads of
state, politicians, and diplomats assassinated in just the first
13 years of the century. The reason the Archduke's murder
sparked off a wider conflagration, Ferguson says, was that the
whole region was sitting on a major geopolitical fault line. Just
as tectonic fault lines become the focal point of earthquakes,
Bosnia and Herzegovina was the fault line between the Occi-
dent and the Orient.

This was a time when most of Europe was dominated and
influenced by old empires that presided over ethnically mixed
populations. The idea of the nation state—where the 'repub-
lic' subsumed regional and ethnic identities—was still in its
infancy. It was this flux that created volatile fault lines among
communities ranging from Europe to the Far East. World War
I (which some historians argue never really ended but merely

tapered before erupting again two decades later) rearranged the world order along new fault lines.

World War II, in turn, morphed into the Cold War and numerous regional conflicts and ethnic clashes that continue to ravage the world to this day. The Indian subcontinent witnessed its share of violent reordering. Over 3.5 million Indian troops—three times the size of the current Indian Army—fought in the two World Wars. The partition of the subcontinent into India and Pakistan, subsequent conflicts involving neighbouring countries in the region, communal riots, and the constant throbbing of disturbed areas like the Kashmir valley and the North-East, indicate underlying fault lines.

The existence of these fault lines is a geopolitical reality and an integral part of terrorists' strategy. Just as small but strategic explosions can wreck a massive superstructure, terrorists leverage the dangerous potential of driving wedges into inherent weak spots, causing them to expand into full-blown fissures.

This aspect has three implications in any counter-terror strategy. First, acts of terror must be seen in terms of the potential they have to exacerbate the overall situation, rather than just as isolated incidents. Viewed from this perspective, the recent assassinations of moderate politicians in Pakistan and their virtual condonation by the establishment result in a widened fracture between fundamentalists and moderates. Similarly, the series of uprisings in the Middle East can alter the influence of radical fundamentalists.

Second, terror itself needs to be redefined. It is a misconception that an act of terror needs to culminate in explosions, hijacks, shootouts, or such high drama. Terror is an instrument of waging war, and war is a continuation of politics by other means. Any act that threatens the sovereignty or well-being of a nation, or causes it to drain resources that would have otherwise been expended on developmental activities, is an act of war. And if this is done by non-state actors or by states in the absence of a formal declaration of hostilities, then it is an act of terror.

Propagators of terror realize the potential of exploiting different streams of damage—from organized crime to organized scams. They do this by interconnecting 'fractures' in different layers of the ecosystem to cause a series of 'explosions', each of which may be labeled as 'crime' but whose cumulative effects are devastating.

Third, the notion that grave threats originate only from established terrorist organizations with sophisticated plans, like the 9/11 attacks, has to be dispelled. Gavrilo Princip was a diminutive individual who was rejected by the Serbian army because of his physical weakness. The assassination attempt that he was part of was bungled from the instant it began. A bomb that the lead conspirator lobbed into the Archduke's open car bounced off, killing bystanders instead. The unharmed Archduke proceeded as per his original schedule, and later decided to visit the injured, who had been admitted to hospital. On the way, his chauffeur happened to take a wrong turn. And by a simple coincidence, Princip, who was buying lunch on the street, found himself facing his intended target.

Hence, it wasn't the intricacy of the plot that sparked off one of the bitterest conflicts in human history. Instead, it was the underlying fault lines that gave way, precipitating into an uncontrollable spiral of events. Counter-terror strategies must, therefore, discern and map the existence of fault lines and their interplay, rather than account for just the incidents and their protagonists.

— ◈ —

Minor Victims of Terrorism

The Beslan massacre showed that terrorists don't spare children. Unfortunately, it may not be the last of its kind

On 1 September, 2004, hundreds of parents underwent a gruesome ordeal in what unarguably ranks as one of the most despicable terrorist attacks of all time. This is the story of the Beslan school massacre and Shamil Basayev, also known as the Osama bin Laden of Russia.

Chechnya, a federal subject of Russia, has had a troubled history since the early 1900s. Historically, Chechens have rebelled several times against Soviet rule, but have always been suppressed by Moscow's iron hand. The Chechen wars in the late 1990s resulted in a series of retaliatory terrorist strikes by Chechen rebels in mainland Russia, killing hundreds of innocent civilians. Basayev, a Chechen insurgent leader, had masterminded many of these killings, including the Moscow theatre attacks in 2002, which resulted in more than 170 deaths.

All over Russia, 1 September marks the start of the new school year, when children celebrate 'Knowledge Day' with their parents and teachers. At 9 a.m. on that day in 2004, when the festivities were in full swing at the school in Beslan, several dozen Chechen rebels armed with automatic weapons, explosives and suicide vests stormed in, and took over 1100 hostages, including 777 children and infants.

The terrorists demonstrated their cruelty within minutes. Twenty men who they considered threats were lined up, shot in cold blood, and their bodies tossed out through the windows. Many were fathers, murdered in front of their children.

The terrorists then herded the hostages into the school's gymnasium, where they were held for the next three days without food and water. The gym was rigged with three independent chains of explosives with multiple triggers, including the 'dead-man's switch'. This is a device that is kept pressed under the feet of a terrorist and is released if he is shot–a strong deterrence against a sudden attack by security forces. The terrorists stripped the hostages of clothes and mobile phones. They also smashed all windows of the school. Both these steps were lessons learnt from the Moscow theatre incident. In that instance, hostages had alerted security forces using their mobile phones, and the latter had pumped in a deadly gas into the theatre before storming it.

By the end of the first day, Russian security forces had cordoned off the Beslan school. But they found it difficult to manage the crowd of over 5000 anxious parents and relatives of the hostages, many of whom were armed and wished to take matters into their own hands. The situation worsened on the second day. The terrorists' demands–including total Russian withdrawal from Chechnya–were impossibly ambitious, and their ruthlessness was exacerbating the situation. Without food, medicines and even water, many hostages resorted to drinking their own urine and children began fainting. Meanwhile, Russian Special Forces, including the elite Alpha unit of the Spetsnaz, took up positions anticipating a storming operation.

The terrorists had been banking on the assumption that Russia's president Vladimir Putin wouldn't dare to put the children's lives on the line–they were certain to be killed in horrendous numbers in any storming operation. The government, on the other hand, could not afford to give in to an act of terror because that could spark off a spate of similar attempts. Adding to the tension were hundreds of armed and increasingly desperate parents who began interfering in the operation. The memory of the Moscow attacks was still fresh, and many were afraid the rescue might be similarly botched.

Also, by the end of the second day, many of the terrorists who were high on drugs were undergoing withdrawal symptoms. They were becoming increasingly violent, threatening hostages and shooting at security forces. Negotiations, too, had broken down, with only a few infants and their mothers being released (one of them refused to leave her two other children behind).

On the third day, all hell broke loose. There are varying accounts of which side triggered the fateful explosion that led to a firefight. But by the end of it, 385 people were dead. Among them were over 180 children. After the three-day ordeal, many of the victims were too weak to even run to safety.

The Beslan massacre has lessons for countries that have to battle terror. First, attacking children demonstrated that terrorists could cross all boundaries. Second, many of the terrorists had no idea that they were going to be killing children; most were high on drugs, and paid scant regard to personal safety. Some of them had been personally affected by the Russian brutalities and were bent on revenge. In such cases, any anti-siege strategy that relies only on responding after the incident or on appealing to the humanity of the attackers through logic or negotiation is bound to fail.

There was, however, a silver lining to the tragedy. In Chechnya and across Russia, people were disgusted and outraged by the incident. Suicide attacks ceased for years. But that was because Chechen terrorism was a state-sponsored tool of waging war against Russia. Such a backlash would not deter non-state actors; it would, in fact, be their objective. Given the vulnerability of children and the potential to instigate blind rage by attacking them, it is an unfortunate reality that Beslan will probably not be the last of such incidents.

— ◈ —

Al Qaeda's 'Turning Move' Tactics

The terrorist outfit and its affiliates have mastered the ability to infiltrate from within and create havoc

In July 1972, a nine-man team of Britain's Special Air Service (SAS) deployed in Oman held out against a band of local rebels for over six hours until they were relieved. Conventional military wisdom advocates an attacking ratio of three to one when assaulting entrenched positions. However, the SAS commandoes held off over 300 men (a ratio of 30 to 1) and beat back several waves of attacks, killing and wounding over 80 of the rebels with a loss of just three of their own.

This incident illustrates the power of Al Qaeda and its affiliates' recent operational strategy in which a small group of terrorists infiltrates or blasts their way inside a fortified garrison and then fights from within—inside out. This is the tactics used by the terrorists in Kashmir, by the Mumbai attackers, and now the attackers of the Mehran naval air base in Pakistan. In military parlance, the manoeuvre is loosely comparable to the 'turning move', which can be implemented at a tactical level as in these instances or at a strategic level.

The essence of a 'turning move' is to force the defender to turn his defences away from its original anticipated direction, thus changing their strength into weakness. The Al Qaeda fighters have now mastered the ability to infiltrate a defensive position and fight outward rather than attacking the position from outside in—tactics preferred by guerillas such as Naxalites, who rely on overwhelming numbers to smother their (usually isolated) target from multiple directions.

This is clever operational strategy by Al Qaeda for many reasons. One, military bases and critical locations are well protected against full-blown conventional attacks, and require large number of terrorists and heavy-weapons support to subdue. Then, amassing such numbers in urban locations would be impossible, as urban militants need to be sophisticated to move or blend into the crowds. Hence the Al Qaeda/Lashkar-e-Taiba (LeT) assembly line produces a different cadre of terrorists, who are trained for 'single-use' suicide missions that they are not expected to survive.

The Mehran base attack in Pakistan, essentially, reversed the SAS stand by infiltrating a group of terrorists inside a well fortified defensive position, and then wreaking havoc from within the complex; successfully holding off repeated attacks from Pakistani forces and elite units such as the Special Services Group for over 17 hours. During this time, they could destroy strategic assets such as the Orions and by extrapolation would also have had enough time to destroy or capture assets, including nuclear weapons.

Recent Al Qaeda/affiliates' strategy seems to favour the 'turning move' even at the policy level. Historically, terrorist organizations have a tacit understanding of not carrying their battles into the region they regard as a base. In turn, the host state provides them assistance and sanctuary or at the very least looks the other way.

As Bruce Riedel, security adviser to four US presidents, observes, the Inter-Services Intelligence, especially under former Pakistan president Zia-ul-Haq, created region-specific terrorist factions. Abdullah Yusuf Azzam, the father of the modern global Islamic jihad—and a major influence on Osama bin Laden—was encouraged to create the Markaz-ud-dawa-wal-Irshad (MDI), whose purpose was to transfer the skills learnt in the Afghan war into Kashmir. The militant wing of MDI went on to become one of the most brutal terror groups focusing on India. The deadly entourage Azzam cultivated included Osama; Khalid Sheikh Mohammed, the brain behind 9/11;

Abu Musab Al-Zarqawi, the leader of Al Qaeda in Iraq, and even leaders from as far as Indonesia such as Riduan Isam-uddin who was later responsible for the Bali bombings.

The largely autonomous tribal areas of Pakistan gradually turned into a melting pot of global jihad with thousands of eager recruits pouring in from an estimated 43 countries, being trained and routed to carry out terrorist activities across the globe. Initially Pakistan itself was spared other than the odd attack on the more liberal politicians. But this situation changed after 9/11 when Pakistan switched loyalties with the very nation whom the jehadis abhorred.

The Al Qaeda and its affiliates realized that Pakistan provid-ed all the elements needed to accelerate terror from within the region that created and nurtured it.

In Pakistan, they have a teetering country, a society with deep schisms, but united in their obsession with India. A geopoliti-cally advantageous location, a fragmented military and, above all, potential access to nuclear devices. In short, the perfect environment for fomenting chaos. Al Qaeda's overarching objective is to precipitate a deadly spiral of destabilizing events that force either the US's or India's hands into the regional powder keg. And the way to achieve this could be further attacks on Pakistani nuclear-asset locations or another outrage like Mumbai. If the US was sufficiently jittery about the possi-bility of loss of Pakistani control over the nuclear assets or India was sufficiently provoked, then the region could well go into a free fall, taking the globe with it.

And while all stakeholders, including Pakistan, must obviously work hard to prevent such occurrences, it would be prudent for India to create an environment which allows its neighbour to focus on eliminating internal threats rather than worrying about its western border.

— ◆ —

The Logic of Suicide Killing

A suicide bomber is a very good option in terms of
returns on investment and costs incurred by his patrons

Hassan Salame ran a macabre operation until his arrest in
1996. A 26-year-old bomb maker, he was tasked by Hamas to
carry out a spate of suicide attacks in Israel as revenge for the
assassination of another legendary predecessor Yahya Ayyash
with the honorific title of 'the engineer'. Salame's bombs were
responsible for killing over 50 innocent civilians before he was
incarcerated.

When we picture individuals who strap on explosives,
mingle among innocent women and children before blowing
their victims into shreds, perhaps the first thought that springs
to mind is: 'What kind of men would do something like this?'
Understandably it is tempting to think of suicide bombers as
evilly deranged persons with no emotions or compunctions.
Unfortunately, that kind of thinking prevents us from understanding their psyche and countering them.

Suicide attacks—or missions in which the attacker's death is
central to the objective—are nothing new. Such attacks have
always formed the toolkit of asymmetric war i.e., where one
side is substantially weaker than its opponent. While the Japanese kamikaze pilots and the German Waffen-SS were possibly
the more celebrated groups of soldiers who used their body as
a bomb, instances of self-sacrifice have been found in virtually
every culture, mythology, and army. And given that terrorism
is essentially an asymmetric war, suicide attacks have been the
favoured strategy of almost all terror groups regardless of ideology or cause. And for good reasons.

Take Al Qaeda, for example. The initial core purpose of
Al Qaeda was to drive the Russians out of Afghanistan. To
achieve this objective, Osama bin Laden had organized his

troops into large tribal bands of hundreds of fighters. For some of the larger convoy ambushes, the Mujahideen—as they were known then—collaborated in groups numbering thousands. However, immediately after 9/11, Al Qaeda knew that the US wrath would not be long in coming. And by the time the US war machine carpet-bombed Tora Bora, the headquarters of Al Qaeda, Osama and bulk of his guerillas had slipped into the tribal areas of Pakistan and dispersed into much smaller units. With allied forces in hot pursuit, Osama realized that the new avatar of Al Qaeda and its affiliate movements had to use a franchise model wherein he would provide the ideological and technical support and the local terror groups were free to choose their own targeting strategy and tactics.

Suicide attacks proved to be the equalizer for several reasons. For one, a suicide bomber is the best option in terms of returns on investment. It takes many months and elaborate infrastructure to train conventional terrorists. For instance, the Mumbai attackers had to undergo months of training in weapons, navigation, communication and, of course, seamanship. The 10 attackers were selected from scores of others who had to be put through similar training. A London-style attack, however, just needs a few hours of training in the actual operation of the bomb. In many instances in Gaza and the West Bank, the bombers are instructed literally a few hours before the detonation.

For another, assembling a team of motivated persons, hiding them, infiltrating them under secrecy is more difficult than a revenge-crazed or glory-hunting individual. Nasra Hassan, a Pakistani journalist who specialized in covering suicide bombers, reported that Hamas' major problem was turning away hordes of young men who clamoured to be accepted for suicide attacks.

Thirdly, they are the poor man's version of a precision-guided smart bomb. While a random explosion itself causes terror, strategic targeting such as the assassination of Rajiv Gandhi and Benazir Bhutto has game-changing potential. Finally, the concept of suicide as a form of attack has an element of chilling terror to it. Once a few suicide attacks have taken place, there is a sense of dread in the target community and they start viewing every strange face with suspicion, especially since most bombers are literally 'boys next door'. The sheer inability of discerning any telltale sign from such 'deranged' persons is a frightening thought especially for countries that possess the technical wherewithal to detect the slightest military movement half way across the world.

Unfortunately, these are but a few reasons why suicide attackers will continue to proliferate. Suicide attacks increased from 81 in 2001 to 460 in 2005 and this growth continues unabated. Ironically the iron-hand tactics used during reprisals to suicide attacks propel a fresh crop of volunteers, exacerbating the problem instead of solving it.

Countries are confronted with a paradigm shift in forms of attack that require conceptual rethinking of response. As Jerrold Post, the founder director of the Center for Analysis of Personality and Political Behavior at the Central Intelligence Agency, points out that since terrorism is essentially psychological warfare, countering them with bombs and missiles is not enough. For every terrorist killed, 10 more spring up enthusiastically. The response to psychological warfare is ironically psychological warfare, but as Post points out, terrorist groups leverage sophisticated media and communication strategy, whereas nation-states haven't even begun to think on those lines.

— ◈ —

Terrorism: Death by Design

The real key to countering terror lies in addressing its psychological impact in a sustained manner

In July, 2011, Mumbai and the country resonated with yet another terror attack. Thirty-one months after 26/11, explosions killed and maimed people and changed the lives of hundreds—forever.

My sense is that apart from the victims and their families, the rest of India will pick up the threads where we left them 31 months ago and move on. And without being judgemental, that is also a response to terrorism. But the problem is that we have started equating 'explosions' and 'bombs' as the only qualifiers of terrorism and view the intermediate period as somehow being 'terror-free'.

It is time to step back and examine just exactly what terrorism is.

When two (or more) countries, communities, ethnicities or even individuals contest for the same resources in a hostile manner, there is conflict. These resources could be material such as land, water, oil, access to ports, or abstract ideas such as ideology and beliefs. However, the fundamental driver of conflict is depleting resources with increasing contenders. All war is essentially to control or obtain resources for one's own communities. Whenever there is war, there will be at least two sides, and usually one will be weaker in some sphere or the other.

Wars are not won by size alone and history is replete with instances of much bigger countries being defeated by smaller ones like the first Sino-Japanese war in which the Japanese Imperial Army routed an army three times its size. Wars are won—or lost—by destroying the opponent's resolve and by making them expend disproportionately more resources than oneself. This is the essence of war.

Terrorism is the favoured weapon of the numerically small-er for the same reasons. The strategic objective of terror is 'disproportionate compellence'. That is, a smaller side is able to compel a much larger opponent to expend disproportion-ate resources and mindshare. And terror as a tool is able to achieve this objective because it is a psychological weapon. Terror is not about absolute loss. It is about the ability to cause that loss in a completely arbitrary manner even if that is much lesser in magnitude.

For instance, India ranks second in the world for natural disasters. India leads the world with 220 snakebite deaths every day. Just two weeks ago we lost 67 lives in a train acci-dent, three times the fatalities of the Mumbai bombing. Yet, Mumbai dominates our mindshare. That's the power of terror. Terror isn't about removed statistical logic, it is about personal emotional panic.

Terror scares us. The grave danger is that it scares us in conti-nuity. On 22 May, 2010, an Indian Airlines plane crashed in Mangalore killing over 200 people. Within days, flights were back to normal traffic. You probably flew in a plane in the aftermath without really worrying about it. We have a similar attitude towards a train accident. Because those are random, seemingly uncontrollable instances. But a terror strike evokes a very different response because of a 'controlled by someone else' feel to it. A hijacker holding hostages creates an eerie provocation deep within us. That causes us to respond far in excess of the resources spent by the terrorists. That compelled resource drain is the true objective of terror.

When you buy a coffee in a five star hotel, you also pay for the enhanced security apparatus that has been implemented post-26/11. That is perpetual terror. Millions of our educated and trained youth stand guard with rifles in what is an economically unproductive activity. That is terror.

When I see four-year-old children raising their arms to be frisked while entering a mall, I see the success of terror every day. Terror has the potential to change our social psyche perpetually because it is death by design. So the real key to countering terror lies in addressing the psychological impact of terror. And that has to be done by addressing the issue across society in a participative and sustained manner.

As an analogy, treating an accident victim requires urgent trauma therapy, but improving a society's health requires structural developments in areas such as education, hygiene, nutrition, vaccinations, investing in medical colleges and hospitals etc. Long-term different tracks that need to work in synchronized ratios. By the same logic, countering terror also requires many long-term tracks spreading across society's different structures to make any meaningful progress. And this is where our focus should be during the periods between attacks. Unfortunately, we focus on the trauma therapy and leave it at that.

Here is an old adage that has served combat leaders well. The more you sweat in peace, the less you bleed in war. The thing is we are already at war. And now might be the time to roll up our sleeves and work up a little sweat—rather than just shedding tears of angst.

Four Pieces of
the Terror Jigsaw

Countering terrorism today requires a systemic response
and not knee-jerk reactions to emergent situations

The attack in Mumbai on 13 July, 2011 heralded the return
of terrorism after a hiatus of 31 months. As usual, there was
a blend of anger, exasperation, and effort to demonstrate
speedy response in abundance, after the attack. The idea that
an immediate response could substitute the development of
a framework to augment counter-terror capability was also
visible. Experts called in by the media bemoan delays in
procurement of equipment and weapons, the breakdown of
human intelligence apparatus, delays in police reforms or
deficiencies in technical intelligence capabilities as the root
causes of the present situation. While the proponents of each
of these aspects are right, of course, the point being missed is
that none of them is mutually exclusive to the other.

A reactive and piecemeal approach to capability improve-
ment—showing some 'action' in consumption of funds, build-
up of equipment and manpower—is inherently suboptimal
from an outcomes perspective. And here is the reason why.

Capability enhancement is the sum total of different streams
working in synergy rather than development of any or all of
them in isolation. Given that the objective of terrorism is to
coerce the mindshare of masses—that should be the end from
where we begin fixing the framework. Whether we have 5,000
CCTV cameras or as many bullet-proof jackets as there are
policemen is irrelevant in wresting back the initiative from
terrorists who will simply find places where there are no
cameras or, for that matter, blow themselves up on camera.

To make a meaningful difference, four thrust lines of counter-
terror strategy need to be developed in conjunction. These

are human intelligence, technical intelligence, infrastructure capacity and most importantly addressing the mindshare of the masses. None of these is more or less important than the others and achieving high capability in even three of them does not improve the overall outcome significantly. All four are equally important.

Human intelligence is unarguably the bedrock of any counter-terror strategy, but is fraught with limitations. The notion that revival of the beat constable will fill a major gap in information gathering is misplaced in the modern urban context, the main theatre of operations in terrorism. The relevance of the beat constable or any other means of gathering information with 'an ear to the ground' has undergone a dramatic change because of the 'verticalization' and 'virtualization' of urban India. A decade ago, policemen on the ground could gather information because their beat was horizontal. People needed to meet physically to communicate and the policeman or his surrogate informant could dip into that stream of information flow. With increased vertical urbanization, the bulk of the policeman's beat has moved out of his orbit. A beat constable has relevance in the horizontal colonies of south Delhi, not in the 30-storey condominiums that are the new paradigm of urbanization.

Secondly, the proliferation of various communication tools is drying up sources on ground. People don't need to meet to exchange information or ideology. That has now moved to the Internet and electronic platforms. Reliance on technical intelligence by itself is also an overrated delusion. Picking out conversations from cyberspace and homing into terrorist cells by triangulating their cellphones make for good movies and sales pitches, but the reality is far more laborious and unyielding. Incredible volume of data is being created every second and the ability to sift through billions of fragments of information is like looking for the proverbial needle in a haystack. Added to this, is the fact that most data in India is still undigitized and, therefore, computationally unsearchable—such data has to substantially be cleansed before any meaningful insights can be tweaked from it. The need to build frameworks and the ecosystem to leverage technical intelligence may be inevitable, but it is a long haul fraught with contradictory requirements of national security and democratic rights of citizens.

Developing infrastructure capacity is perhaps the most complex of the four pillars because, ironically, every rupee that we spend in increasing our counter-terror infrastructure is a victory for the terrorists. Plucking Osama bin Laden from his lair was a major triumph for the US, but let us not be deluded that Osama did not have his share of spoils too. Al Qaeda's strategy of 'bleeding to bankruptcy' is forcing the US to cut back several developmental activities and has contributed in no small measure to its financial crisis.

Each time we lobby for the procurement of more hardware and weapons or the raising of forces we are walking down the road the terrorists want us to. We currently protect hotels, marketplaces, temples, offices, headquarters, airports, railway stations, among others. Soon it would be schools, campuses, universities and personalities. Before we realize it, our cities will turn into garrisons causing resource drains diverted from developmental activities, exacerbating further dissent.

— ◆ —

Terrorism, Some Lessons from Medicine

If terrorism is to be scaled back, its appeal to those who are vulnerable to its 'charm' has to be understood

In September, 2011, addressing a United Nations symposium on counterterrorism, Britain's home secretary, Theresa May, underlined the need to address terrorism beyond the remit of the military and police. She emphasized the need to address the ideology and, more importantly, the need to understand terrorism's appeal, before being able to counter it.

Britain has long been the home for radical ideologues and proponents of terrorism. Well before the London bombings—which were essentially carried out by homegrown players—the country has and continues to be a proving ground for thousands of radicals who preach, recruit, plan and, on occasions, execute terrorist plots. It has a large concentration of Al Qaeda supporters and London produces a disproportionate number of the world's known terrorists—earning it the sobriquet Londonistan.

Increasingly, research has shown that radicalization occurs because marginalized people search for a sense of identity, meaning and belonging. In a sense, terrorist organizations do not recruit terrorists—the terrorists recruit themselves and the organization just channels a perceived sense of injustice (whether justified or not) into a concrete and often devastating action plan.

Should terrorism then be treated as a social issue rather than just a military or law and order problem? Tina Rosenberg, a Pulitzer Prize winning journalist, argues that countering terrorism has a lot in common with combating several other social problems such as alcoholism, drug abuse, social discrimination, and even improving academic performance among minority students. Her premise is that social pressure or 'peer pressure' has enormous unrecognized potential that can be unleashed using a simple 'unlocking' lever to achieve astounding results.

One of the several examples in her book 'Join the Club' illustrates using the power of social pressure in combating tuberculosis (TB)—a disease that kills over two million people each year. Ironically, the cure for TB is fairly straightforward, requiring just four doses of antibiotics costing a few hundred rupees. However, the course of treatment needs to run over nine months and this is where most patients slip. Even if one dose is missed—which is often the case, because either the patient has stopped coughing or because of the unpleasant side effects of the medicine—the strain of TB becomes drug-resistant and highly virulent, necessitating treatment in thousands of dollars, well out of the reach of majority of the victims.

Because of the long duration of the cure and the deadly implication of stopping earlier, adherence to the drug dosage regime was key to the successful TB treatment, which was literally forced upon the patients. In 1950s, however, a new strategy was developed (in India) that was called DOTS—directly observed treatment, short course. While DOTS had several components to it, the key was that someone directly observed the patient swallowing his medicine. This could be a nurse, community health worker, or even a family member.

DOTS improved cure rates by over 40 percent. It seemed that individuals who would not take medicines on their own would take it when made accountable to a peer.

The key word, however, in all of Rosenberg's examples is 'peer': someone from within the community—not an outsider or an official.

Britain's home office seems to recognize this aspect when they appeal for action from non-governmental organizations,

civil society, and other faith groups in countering the influence of extremists who present a prejudiced view to potential
recruits. The country's counterterrorism strategy lays emphasis
on assisting individuals who are vulnerable to radicalization
and on enrolling participation of institutions such as schools,
religious establishments, universities, and even prisons in
furthering an unbiased and factual implication of terrorist acts.

A key challenge we have in India is the sheer scale, diversity and remoteness of the country and, therefore, its threats.
While resource-rich countries such as the US and Britain have
to deal with just one or two forms of terrorism, we have a
whole range of internal security issues and an apparatus that
is ill-equipped to administer the social cure methodology.
Besides, successful social cure experiments must be spearhead-
ed from within society and not imposed on it by government
machinery. The content of the message is not as important as
who delivers it and how.

But we may have an answer in the form of our ex-servicemen
from the police, paramilitary, and defence forces. In them, we
have millions of trained and disciplined personnel in every
nook and corner of India. Professionals who understand
national security and can discern anti-national activities at the
grass-roots level. They are used to operating in a command and
control structure and are respected peers within their local
communities, more so because of their 'country first—caste/reli-
gion/self later' exemplar ethos. If we could start a programme
to harness the potential of this incredible pool of committed and motivated resources, India can permeate a change in
the way society recognizes the need for social participation in
discerning and addressing internal security issues at the bud.

— ◈ —

Children of a Lesser God

Using children as soldiers is morally unacceptable. But
terrorist groups and 'freedom fighters' think otherwise

The most reprehensible aspect of low intensity conflicts such
as insurgencies, irregular warfare, and terrorism is also one of
the least known—the use of children as soldiers.

Civilized societies—as also civilized readers—would cringe at
the thought of children as young as eight years being used as full-
fledged combatants. Yet this scourge is perpetuated by several
'revolutionaries', terrorist organizations and, sadly, even some
states. As Romeo Dallaire, a former Canadian peacekeeper with
experience in Africa, points out, a child soldier is the ultimate
end-to-end weapon system in the inventory of war machines,
proven by its use in scores of conflicts all over the world.

Children have been used in genocides such as Rwanda—where
800,000 people were slaughtered in just 100 days—and by the
Khmer Rouge in Cambodia. Child soldiers have been thrown
into combat against battle-hardened Soviet soldiers by the
Afghan mujahideen, against the Indian Army by the Liberation
Tigers of Tamil Eelam (LTTE) and against the allied troops in
Iraq and Afghanistan. Children have been routinely used to
clear mine fields by making them walk ahead of adult soldiers,
as pack animals to carry supplies and even as suicide bombers.

Villages in Rwanda, Congo, Cambodia, Sri Lanka, and
several other countries have been slaughtered by warlords with
the objective of 'harvesting' children. Girls, who constitute up
to 40 percent of child soldiers in certain countries, are especially prized because, in addition to all the things that boys can
do, they are useful for cooking, cleaning, as sex slaves and, in
some horrifying situations, to produce the next generation of
child soldiers.

To a lesser degree, we also have our share of this horror in insurgencies in the North-east, the Naxalite movement and, of course, in countless cases of organized crime ranging from drug dealing, begging, smuggling, prostitution to forced labour.

If one overcomes the repugnancy of the idea, it is easy to see why children are used in conflicts. They are available in plentiful numbers, especially in continents such as Africa and Asia. They can be coerced into absolute submission using tools of fear and violence such as beating, mutilation, rape, and execution—often at the hands of peers. Most of the children are orphaned, often by the very warlords who abuse them, and in that fearful daze, they transfer their loyalty to their kidnappers. Crazed with hunger, terror and drugs, they have no sense of humanity or compassion and, therefore, are capable of incredible cruelty and violence. Their role models are older children who have become leaders in the groups by displaying those very qualities.

They cost less to 'maintain', don't need to be paid and never question their orders, no matter how repugnant. Children arouse less suspicion, so they can be used for gathering information and entering well-guarded positions where adults would probably be stopped and searched. This is a favoured tactic, especially in insurgencies, making troops jittery about the presence of children. Lastly, even battle-hardened soldiers find it extremely hard to consider children as enemy combatants and hesitate to fire at them. In operations, that hesitation provides a tactical advantage to insurgents and demoralizes regular troops that feel repulsive about fighting children.

The LTTE, for instance, used children successfully against the Indian Peace Keeping Force, and in a macabre twist had created 'Bakuts' or baby brigades, consisting children between

10 and 16 years of age and 'Sirsu Puli', or leopard brigades, consisting entirely of orphans.

The United Nations estimates that over six million children have been permanently disabled, over two million have been killed, and over a quarter of million are being used in conflicts as combatants in over 30 countries. In most instances, this essentially destroys the community's capability to rebuild itself and leaves an entire generation psychologically and emotionally scarred.

It is only in the last decade or so that the international community has begun to tackle the issue in a meaningful way. In the International Conference on War-Affected Children in Winnipeg, Canada, in September 2000, concrete steps were recommended that included providing amnesty to child soldiers, special emphasis on rehabilitating them and urging governments to eradicate the unfettered supply of small arms as this is a major factor in the proliferation of child soldiers.

There are an estimated 650 million small arms in conflict zones, with responsible developed countries adding a million more each year. The five permanent members of the UN Security Council (China, Russia, France, Britain, and the US) continue to be the world's largest weapons producers.

With a burgeoning child population, both in absolute terms as well as those involved in conflicts and crime, India has a long way to go in addressing this issue. Our recognition and acknowledgement of the problem and the resources allocated to preventing abuse of children and their rehabilitation are minuscule. As a country, we must realize the cost that the society will have to pay if we don't rescue these ravaged children from conflicts, crime, and abuse. And at an individual level, we ought to remember that, but for the grace of God, that devastated child could have been ours.

— ◈ —

The Devil's Alternative

Political leaders often face 'lose-lose' decisions, but we must allow them to make choices and appreciate them

On 4 July, 1976, 106 Israeli commandos flew 4,000 km into Entebbe in Uganda, where Palestinian and German Palestine Liberation Organization (PLO) sympathizers were holding Israeli hostages. Within 90 minutes of landing, they killed all seven hijackers and freed all but one of the 103 hostages. For good measure, the commandos also killed 45 Ugandan soldiers who were obstructing them and destroyed 30 aircrafts of the Ugandan air force. The raid led by Col Yonatan Netanyahu is considered one of the most daring military operations for its audaciousness, planning, and ruthless execution. (Incidentally, Netanyahu was the only fatality among the commandos and was the elder brother of Benjamin Netanyahu, who became Israel's prime minister.) Operation Thunderbolt, as it was known, went a long way in creating the feared reputation of Israeli response to hostage-taking.

However, in the past decades, Israel has also exchanged over 7,000 prisoners to retrieve just 19 soldiers and eight dead bodies. The last of such exchanges happened in October, 2011 when Gilad Shalit, captured by Hamas in 2006, was exchanged for 1,027 PLO prisoners languishing in Israeli jails. That is right, over 1,000 captured prisoners—some of them highly dangerous—were released for just one soul by the same country whose daring raid on Entebbe has never been surpassed.

This seemingly dichotomous behaviour highlights challenges of formulating a textbook 'policy' to deal with crises such as hijacking or hostage taking. A potent tool of terror—taking of hostages is actually a psychological weapon. More than the lives of the hostages themselves, it is the seeming helplessness of the authorities which the terrorists seek to exploit. If the authorities stand fast and refuse to succumb, they are viewed as callous and heartless. On the other hand, capitulating to demands paints them as cowardly and spineless and incentivizes other such attempts. It is the ultimate devil's alternative.

Political leaders often face such 'lose-lose' decisions where the objective is to minimize damage, rather than maximize benefits. Winston Churchill, as a newly elected prime minister, faced his devil's alternative during World War II in the summer of 1940. Hitler's armies were steamrolling over Europe. Poland, Denmark, Norway, the Netherlands, and Belgium had capitulated and France was teetering on the brink. Over 150,000 British troops were still stranded in the continent and the Nazi army was creeping closer each day. The US had still not joined the war and in fact, Joseph Kennedy, the US ambassador to Britain, strongly argued against giving aid to Britain. Britain stood alone against the juggernaut of the Third Reich.

Churchill, Neville Chamberlain, and Lord Halifax huddled for four days to debate an offer of mediation by Mussolini on behalf of Hitler. Churchill finally decided not to negotiate and on 4 June, 1940, went out to his nation with his most famous speech 'We shall fight on the beaches...we shall never surrender.'

Nelson Mandela, on the other hand, was a leader who chose to negotiate. While serving a sentence of 20 years for treason, he took the unilateral decision to negotiate with his captors without even consulting his compatriots in jail or the then leader of the African National Congress (ANC)—Oliver Tambo.

In hindsight, both leaders took decisions that were unimaginable at the time. The entire British army was trapped in Dunkirk, and almost all their equipment, tanks, and guns had been lost. The US was in no mood to get involved in the continental war and there was a very real threat of capitulation of the island. Hitler seemed to offer immunity to Britain and retention of its colonies as he was focusing on expansion into eastern and southern Europe. And yet Churchill refused to negotiate.

Mandela's decision to negotiate was equally incredible because of the long history of bitter violence of the anti-apartheid struggle and also especially because Mandela was the founder and the head of the armed wing of ANC which was directly responsible for several terrorist acts, such as the 'Church Street Bombing'. Nonetheless, he led his party into negotiations over four years and went on to become the president of South Africa and the joint recipient of the Nobel Peace Prize along with his predecessor F.W. de Klerk.

Harvard professor Robert Mnookin points out the underlying dilemma of such situations in his aptly titled book *Bargaining with the Devil*. Negotiating in a lose-lose situation often involves some sacrifice of principle in favour of practicality and decision makers have to, therefore, rely on what is best in the long term rather than the immediate crisis. In the age of terrorism, hostage taking will become a recurring reality.

Perhaps a policy for dealing with it could be found in the rationale that Churchill gave Lord Halifax who was in favour of negotiating with Hitler. Churchill argued that the spirit of British populace was still holding strong. If they learnt that their leadership was forced into negotiations, morale would plummet and if negotiations failed—and there was good chance of that, then as a wartime prime minister; rallying them again would be formidable for him.

In many ways, the policy in such situations should be to allow the leadership on the spot to make choices and appreciate that they may have reasons which only history can judge. For sometimes, leadership is not about making a decision between a right and a wrong—instead it is about choosing between a right and another right.

— ◆ —

Shaping Opinion via Spam

India needs a robust cyber defence strategy to stop this new 'weapon of mass destruction'

In May, 2012, India beat the US to become the highest relayer of spam mail globally. This dubious ignominy reinforces the economic damage spam and other such malicious mails cause. For most of us, unwarranted mails promising goodies are just an irritant. But obvious scams such as inheritances in Nigeria or winning lotteries continue flooding the inbox because people fall for such cons with alarming gullibility.

Over the last few years, spam mail has outnumbered 'legit' mail. Most people think of spam as rip-offs which solicit money; but they are far more lethal. To begin with, spams waste a more valuable resource—time—spent in watching pulp philosophy presentations or manually sifting through them. They also choke the Internet bandwidth and mailboxes in desktops and servers. Also, every time such mails are forwarded by well-intending people, the network explodes into a ping pong of a million unnecessary packets clogging up the entire grid.

Since such mails do not have a singular recipient or an action that can end the chain, they continue perpetually in the expanses of the cyber world. Many of the mails are deliberately crafted to 'grow' in number. Such mails extol the user to forward them to others or else terrible luck awaits them! In a nation which believes that stone idols consume milk, perpetual proliferation of spam is thus ensured. This means the sender also forwards the entire list of the previous recipients' mail IDs to everyone on their own distribution list, thus enabling 'harvesting' identities of genuine and often socially similar individuals. The latter ploy is a sociological ingenuity as many messages are crafted to titillate a particular community—for instance, defence forces, expats, bureaucrats, scientists, students, etc. This allows development of powerful databases that are used to identify socially influential subgroups and precision bomb them with specifically developed 'sales' pitches.

While the obvious and the prevalent usage seems to be for commercial value propositions, such mails can also be used to shape opinion. Studies have shown that multiple exposures to false messages, interspersed with facts, start to shape beliefs that are untrue. Such opinion-shaping tools can also be used to spread insidious allusions about individuals, companies, policy positions, or even undermining the confidence of a nation by propagating a sense of disarray and dismay. In the Twitter era, readers seldom ascertain the genuineness of information received from the Internet. More importantly, the human brain is incapable of 'remembering' the veracity factor of information stored in its long-term memory. So regardless of the number of citations or references, or the lack of them, most information is processed with the same degree of belief or disbelief; but seldom in shades between.

Such powerful usages are already seen among that most ingenious group of all—terrorists and in some cases, even state entities. Harvesting of targeted profiles allows focused indoctrination with much better success rates of conversion. It also helps strategically because groups indoctrinated in the same geographic location or communities act as ready-made buddies with less chances of detection. There is after all, safety in numbers, (albeit small numbers). Once recruited to the cause, such cadre can be trained online in a variety of sabotage and subterfuge. Al Qaeda has detailed films on the Internet that teach novices how to build suicide vests and the suggested targeting methodology to get maximum physical and psycho-logical impact, among other such chilling recipes.

Other mails carry dangerous payloads in the form of customized programmes designed to bypass anti-virus software and cause damage. It is well-known that our adversaries have sophisticated cyber warfare initiatives which alarm even countries such as the US which spend far more on their cyber defence programmes than India can ever imagine. The ability to take out even nuclear reactors using a software worm moved from realms of fiction into harsh reality in 2010 when Iranian centrifuges ground to a halt. Incidentally India is the third-most affected country by the same worm behind Iran and Indonesia.

Contrary to what software salesmen say, there is no silver bullet for such serious risks. The filters and other heuristic firewalls can certainly sieve some such attacks, but custom-crafted ones get through them. Subscriptions to newsletters, advertisements and most certain of all; that forwarded mail from a friend, all find their way to eyeballs. The only comprehensive defence against such attacks is, of course, a robust cyber defence strategy with systematic education and awareness. This is a major challenge for a country which is embarking on a multitude of e-governance projects and requires to train millions of users on the basics of computing and collaborative working. In addition, proliferation of hand-held devices, wireless networks and introduction of 4G bandwidth will just explode the number of vulnerable devices and users unless a national strategy co-opting the state, companies and private citizens is put in place rapidly. As other countries are realizing, such strategies need to get the cooperation of stakeholders rather than merely issuing missives or guidelines, because they have a direct impact on the bottom line and cause major inconveniences. And none of that can begin unless the stakeholders realize the looming danger of this new weapon of mass destruction.

— ◆ —

The Kasab Factories

In his book *The Man Who Laughs*, Victor Hugo introduced the hideous vocation of 'Comprachios'—the 'Child Buyers'. This tribe bought or kidnapped infants, and then deliberately mutilated them. They would break their spines, joints of the limbs, slit their eyelids and an assortment of other disfigurements to create human monsters that were sold to kings to serve as mountebanks. This deliberate mutilation of the body and mind was also practised in China where children were dwarfed – much like bonsai by putting them inside Ming vases for years, deforming and stunting their growth to serve as court jesters. But in recent times this gruesome model is refined to create an army of foot soldiers of which Kasab was, but just one example.

In 2010, Pakistani filmmaker Sharmeen Omaid won an Emmy for her remarkable film, *The Children of Taliban*, which documents the five-step methodology of the extremist organization's assembly line to create suicide bombers. Step one begins with targeting poor and rural families from whom the children are taken with promises of food and education to hardline training schools hundreds of miles away.

The second is intense indoctrination based on a corrupted interpretation of the Koran with a complete blackout of all other information. The third step is to make these children hate the world and their own existence by meting out inhuman treatment like frequent beatings, being fed twice a day on bread and water, and being kept as virtual prisoners.

The fourth step is to brainwash them by promising glory in the afterlife. Of the lakes of milk, honey, and 72 virgins. Of the honour they bring to their families and tutors with their mission. Compared to their subhuman conditions—death seems like redemption. And the final step is Taliban's forte of propaganda. The children are shown skewed and doctored videos and pictures of purported atrocities on Muslims around the world by the West and India. They are now ready to blow themselves up with no inkling of the elaborate manipulation.

Transcripts of Kasab's interrogation and intercepts of his handlers show evidences of a similar training model. There is frequent reference to the glory of Islam, insistence on not getting caught alive, constant urging to keep killing as many people as possible and of course the promise of heavenly rewards. Kasab and his accomplices' profiles fit the model perfectly. Poor, rural, uneducated with no recognition of the grievous nature of their actions or its consequences. They are cannon fodder and there are plenty more where they came from.

This is why India should treat Kasab's execution as a routine wrap up rather than some 'closure' that it is being perceived as. The factories which produce Kasabs are very much in existence and will continue for good reasons. Firstly, they are impossible to completely 'destroy', even if the host country wanted to. These are schools which require a piece of hinterland, some basic assault weapons, a couple of instructors and indoctrinators and of course, expendable students of which there is no shortage.

Second, this model is unparalleled for its return on investment. Let alone the damage caused by Kasab and co, even keeping him alive to go through legal requirements cost the exchequer hundreds of crores. Thirdly and most alarmingly, this assembly line does not have any master switch, i.e. there is no central high command that can be coerced or eliminated to stop the production of suicide missionaries. A strategic masterstroke of Taliban Inc. was to franchise this model into literally 'mom and dad' outfits. A handful of people with funding generated through donations or extortions can keep the assembly line alive; requiring very little external support and by corollary, leaving low intelligence footprints.

This essentially means that hanging Kasab—or for that matter keeping him alive—has little significance in the overall scheme of things. The Kasab factories will continue spewing their venomous wards and every affected nation will face this reality. The syllabi and quality of raw material may vary, but 9/11 in the US, 7/7 in UK, and 26/11 in India were all perpetrated by these 'factory' graduates. Tackling these factories or their graduates alone, is a tactical riposte with little benefit.

Instead we must look at strategic options available to us. Going after their leadership is essential but unlikely to yield much. Arguably, India cannot send a hit squad of assassins after them like Israel post the Munich massacre. That's not our DNA and it is a different world from the seventies. Nor do we have the geopolitical clout to execute a liquidation operation like the US did to Osama bin Laden.

However, India has other strategic options that can be game changers. One is to debilitate the 'firm base' providers for terrorists within the country. Kasab and his accomplices could not have conducted such an elaborate operation without local assistance or advance reconnaissance. We simply must create an environment that convinces the terrorists and more importantly their sympathisers of the certainty of being caught. The second is to counter propaganda with a strong communication program of our own, demolishing the brainwashing of the recruiters with facts. Both these steps however require the ability to think strategically and the discipline of execution. And unless we maintain course on this, the noose around Kasab's neck is little more than tying a loose end of a devastating attack on our country.

— ◆ —

Dancing on the Edge

A slow controllable simmer with India is the
Pakistani army's existential need

A popular illustration of game theory goes something like this.
Suppose you are one of five isolated players, each of whom
starts with $100 and a button. The players have one choice
they can make, to push the button or not. Pushing the button
by any player has two consequences. The first is all other players lose $30. This means that, if, say four players pressed the
button, you would lose $120, so you are down $20 as against
the $100 you began with. But pressing the button by any player
has another consequence. And that is, it halves that player's
own losses. So if you too pressed the button, you would lose
only $60 and get to keep $40. And these rules of the game are
common knowledge as every player knows them. Should you
press the button? This seemingly trivial game tells a lot about
human behaviour, motivation and why rational leaders seem
to make irrational decisions.

In an ideal world, no one should press their button and all
five players make $100 each. But it's not an ideal world and
each player can have different motivations. You don't know
the other four players. Can you really trust them? While you
are noble and will do the right thing, what if the others don't
think that way? So if you do push your button, you will still
get $40. Not as good as getting all $100 but definitely better
than losing $20. Or perhaps you don't really care that much
about $100 and would just like to shake things up by pushing
the button. Or you may decide to resist pushing the button
because it is the ethical thing to do (even if you lose $120), as
a mark of good faith because you figure you'll play this game
again. All these decisions seem rational from a certain view

point and yet only one of them allows the full potential of every player's payoff.

Replace the players with countries, the payoffs with self-interests of those countries, trust levels between them with common knowledge and buttons with military conflict and suddenly the game looks far more ominous that merely pushing buttons for dollars.

In January, 2013, Pakistan upped the ante along the Line of Control by mutilating two Indian soldiers. The blame game squared on the Pakistani army, the Inter-Services Intelligence (ISI) or militants, depending on which report one read. But regardless of the perpetrators, it was a provocation that worked. Confidence-building measures faltered and the animosity between the countries was injected with a fresh dose of venom. Political jingoism and rightful indignation notwithstanding, the Pakistani army, ISI, militants, and the Pakistani populace are four different players, each with very different motivations and self-interests. Clubbing them together will result in a flawed strategic response at the very least and possibly a disastrous one, considering that in this game the buttons are nuclear.

Given that Pakistan's gross domestic product (GDP) is barely one-tenth of India's, any military conflagration would irreversibly destroy its already precarious economy, especially since its military is still committed and smarting from heavy engagement in Afghanistan and its own hinterland. Ironically, the group that loses most if the economy nosedives is the Pakistani military high command. This is because of two reasons. One, despite its best packaging efforts as a victory, the Kargil misadventure put Pakistan's military in poor light—having provoked India and got a bloody nose in the bargain. A similar or worse defeat could trigger a major upheaval in their close-ranked organization. Second, and perhaps more paradoxically,

Three Myths of Battling Terrorism

There is no 'magic bullet' cure for terrorism. Without governance reforms, the menace can't be checked

The Hyderabad bombings on 21 February, 2013 ended a spell of inactivity by terrorists and have rekindled demands for action from people who believe that this attack ended a somewhat enduring period of peace. This is a myth. The country was always under attack from terrorists. It is important to understand the strategic dimensions of terrorism, without which, well-meaning demands for action will not only be misdirected but actually abet the aims of terrorists.

Terrorism is the strategic weapon of choice of an adversary that is weaker or chooses a covert mode of war. Decrying terrorism assuages a sense of angst, but does not alter its nature. Several aims of terrorists boil down to a single purpose: To exert influence, far beyond conventional capability of those using this weapon. So when Al Qaeda bombs the US forces out of Afghanistan, or the Lashkar-e-Taiba disrupts normal life or goons prevent the screening of a film by threatening violence—they are all using a strategic weapon that projects influence far beyond their numerical strength. But for terrorism to succeed, its intended target also must respond in a dramatically disproportionate manner. The context in which these groups operate needs to be understood clearly.

India loses millions of lives each year due to preventable diseases, adulterated food, spurious medicines, pollution caused by illegal effluent discharges and simply from the blatant disorganization prevalent across its length and breadth. For instance in 2011, the country lost 186,000 persons in road accidents alone—or over 20 people per hour. And another half a million were wounded.

it is the Pakistani military that controls and benefits from a large chunk of their economy. As Ayesha Siddiqa points out in her book *Military Inc.: Inside Pakistan's Military Economy*, a tiny minority of serving and ex-military officers control a disproportionate quantum of the Pakistani economy. So, rationally speaking, they stand most to lose if the economy teeters, as it undoubtedly will in the event of a conflict. But in many ways the Pakistani army's raison d'être is the myth of a belligerent India and if that is not constantly propped up within its populace, sounder voices would start questioning the political, social, and economic supremacy of the military.

The delicate dance that the Pakistani high command therefore does is to keep tension with India at slow controllable simmer. ISI has decades of experience in using militants for such war of attrition and the exit of the Americans from the region give them the elbow room needed.

Michael Kinsley, a *Washington Post* correspondent, used the following metaphor to describe game theory. Imagine you are chained to another man's ankle while standing on the edge of a cliff. One of you will be released and given a reward if the other gives in. But the only persuasive tool you have for making the other person give in is by threatening to push him off the cliff. But that will doom you too. There is a way out, though. You start dancing closer and closer to the edge of the cliff to convince him that while you may not take an irrational step like pushing him off the cliff, you are prepared to take far larger risks than he is.

And while military leaders who control their country dictatorially can and must do such a dance to survive, democratically elected counterparts shouldn't mimic their foolhardiness and send wrong signals to their populace.

— ◆ —

Estimates by Forbes show this drained 2.7 percent of India's gross domestic product (GDP). In contrast, the country's health budget was a paltry 1.2 percent of GDP in the same period.

The 26/11 Mumbai attackers killed just 166 persons in three days. Yet since then, not only India, but several countries have spent billions of dollars in implementing security precautions to try and prevent a Mumbai-style attack.

Every time you buy a coffee in a hotel, you pay for the security apparatus put in place after the Mumbai attacks. Every time you fly, your ticket costs more to amortize the newly introduced security checks. The security industry has now become the second largest employer in India. These billions of rupees which are diverted from developmental budgets into what is a fundamentally non-productive expenditure is the real terrorist attack—in perpetuity. The aim of our adversaries is to prevent us from achieving our true economic potential and they are succeeding splendidly—simply because we don't realize that our largely (economically) wasteful response to terrorism is the actual attack.

The bluster of 'zero tolerance to terrorism' is the second myth. This line, in itself, literally means nothing. Of course, leaders are duty-bound to assuage terrified citizens and the seriousness with which terrorism is being taken is captured to an extent in this declaration. The problem is that this goal is simply not achievable. As explained earlier, terrorism is a strategy and not an apparatus existing in isolation. There are, of course, training camps where guerilla warfare and terrorist tactics, indoctrination and suicide attacks are taught. But these are tactical measures and cater largely to the last mile. The characteristic of terrorism is that it leverages the very apparatuses it seeks to destroy. Terrorists use public transportation, public communication channels, commercial houses, legitimate and illegitimate fund transfer methods to further their aims.

Consider this. Every day millions of dollars' worth of contraband and spurious goods are smuggled in and out of India. These include spurious automobile parts, medicines, fake branded watches, exclusive label wear, drugs, counterfeit currency, and human trafficking.

This illegal trade flourishes using the very same channels which terrorists can piggyback on without any danger of detection. So the next time you see pirated DVDs being sold in neighbourhood shops or admire a friend's fake Rolex, you are watching the terminal end of a supply chain that could have well been used to transport high explosives, weapons or even terrorists into the country. There is simply no way to achieve zero tolerance to terrorism in an environment that has high tolerance for every other crime.

The last myth of terrorism is that there is a silver closed circuit TV out there which is going to contain or prevent the next attack. The efficacy of terrorism is demonstrated when inexperienced (counter-terror-wise that is) citizens too, pitch in their advice on how to tackle terrorism by buying tools.

Fighting terrorism is best understood through the metaphor of society as a patient and terrorism as a disease. Terrorism is not a tumour that can be surgically removed by a team of well-equipped surgeons with little participation from the society. Instead, it has to be appreciated as a condition that can only be cured through active physiotherapy. The specialists can certainly diagnose, guide and help, but it is the patient who has to methodically carry out the steps that cleanse the body, strengthen and cure it. And just as physiotherapy necessitates traumatic changes in lifestyle, removal of toxins, improved discipline and the rigour of a healthy regimen, terrorism too can only be addressed through fundamental changes in mindset, long-term development of modern institutions, and all-round revamp of governance systems.

Fighting an Asymmetric War

Half the Indian Army is permanently located in Jammu and Kashmir, and many parts of the country have been denied progress for several decades

The paradox facing our army, the third largest in the world, is that it is engaged in many small battles instead of the big decisive one it was meant to fight. Divisions and corps that were structured to punch through the Pakistani defences and scythe deep into enemy hinterlands are hopelessly tied up in resource-draining, high-attrition, and seemingly endless skirmishes inside their own borders.

Welcome to the world of asymmetric warfare!

Our enemies, (who include state and non-state players) had long realized the futility of taking on the juggernaut of the Indian Armed Forces in conventional warfare. After the humiliating 1971 rout, Pakistani military establishment, (the de facto source of the country's political leadership), initiated a doctrine of asymmetric warfare, whose mission was to bleed the Indian military capability by creating and coordinating hundreds of small fighting units employing guerrilla tactics of hitting civilian and vulnerable targets.

The return on investment of this strategy has been excellent. Half the Indian Army is permanently located in Jammu and Kashmir, and many parts of the country have been denied progress for several decades. In this chapter, I want to talk about the lethality of asymmetric warfare and possible solutions.

The two main instruments of asymmetric operations are terrorism and insurgency. They are distinct from each other and need to be tackled differently as well.

Terrorism targets local populace and often selects vulnerable defenceless targets—for example, the attacks in Mumbai. It has four main objectives. Firstly, to terrorize or instil a deep sense of uncertainty and panic. Secondly, to undermine the establishment's ability to protect its citizens. Thirdly, to tie down disproportionate quantum of resources to maintain order and, finally, to provoke the state to react in a heavy handed manner, often against its own citizens. Terrorism is mounted by 'outsiders' unto the community and local support is often coerced or commercially obtained.

Insurgency, on the other hand, is often the manifestation of economic/political deprivation or ideological differences that thrives on active local support and involvement. While terrorists seek to undermine the government by hitting the populace, insurgents strike the government itself.

Their endgame is to make it expensive for the establishment to deny their demands, which could range from greater autonomy to total secession. Insurgency, unlike terrorism, recruits its cadres from within the community and while coercion may exist to some extent, there is underlying support from the society.

The government has some fundamental challenges while dealing with asymmetric warfare. Prime among them is just finding the anti-national elements. Locating terrorists is like looking for a needle in a haystack. For most practical purposes, these elements behave like the citizens they live among. Ironically, democracies are more vulnerable simply because their security establishments don't have inward-looking apparatuses. In any case, this is not a job for the Armed Forces which is designed to destroy an identified enemy, not to identify it in the first place. That requires subtlety and discretion, not force or firepower.

The second challenge is that terrorists can seize initiative at will. They can choose their time and place of attack and need to be lucky just once, whereas state forces cannot anticipate every possible eventuality or protect every potential target. The third and the most debilitating one is unequal distribution of troops required to combat terrorism or insurgency. Thousands of soldiers are routinely haemorrhaged by just a handful of terrorists who can effect stand-offs for days. Combing operations to flush out insurgents can bog down entire divisions.

A meaningful way to alter this disadvantaged détente is a two-pronged strategy; first of which is matching the nimbleness and mobility of the enemy. To do that, the state needs to develop sophisticated intelligence frameworks that connect different socio-economic infrastructures such as banking, travel, communications, the Internet, and residential movements into a singular grid that can discern patterns and proactively predict potential threats.

The second and equally important part of the strategy is to focus on the cause rather than the manifestation. Insurgency's root causes are genuine and long unaddressed. And there are vested interests who want the situation to be status quo. Educating, connecting, and inclusively empowering the stakeholders are key essentials to a long-term solution.

It is time we spent a little less resource on finding enemies and a lot more on finding friends.

A Public-Private Response to Tackle Terror

The private security business is the second largest employer after manufacturing

On 6 August, 2009, *Mint* carried a front page story on 75 companies lining up to avail the services of the Central Industrial Security Force (CISF).

While it is indeed a sign of our times that companies have to pay to get the security that they should have had in the first place, I believe this could be a paradigm shift in the way public-private partnerships address the issue of terrorism and internal security.

The willingness of firms to make investments in security is a heartening sign of their readiness and concern to be active participants rather than passive stakeholders. However, this strategy needs to be thought through its implications and dimensions to be leveraged optimally.

Firstly, companies must realize that CISF or any such force is essentially a quick reaction team. The key word here is reaction. Hence, the police or private security cannot abdicate their responsibility to control, access, or gather pre-emptive intelligence.

Grassroots security and first response will continue to be a police responsibility simply because the police force is closest to the community and can consequently spot weak signals first. Therefore, all initiatives to modernize them with superior intelligence gathering tools and immediate response equipment need to proceed on a fast track.

Secondly, CISF, like any other government force, is already stretched. As a matter of fact, it is yet to cover its current set of responsibilities with national assets such as airports because scaling up and maintaining high quality is a universal challenge.

Also, while the police force intends to augment strength by 10,000 every year, recruiting and churning out such numbers is a daunting task. CISF competes with the same catchment pool as the army and all other paramilitary forces, which are also increasing their strength rapidly.

However, the key issue that must be addressed by the private sector is—security at what cost? It is unarguable that government assets cost the exchequer around three times that of privately provisioned resources.

The private guarding business in India is the second largest employer of manpower after the manufacturing industry. Despite that, most of the guarding companies have an unsavoury reputation and the few that tend to adhere to standards are hobbled by the antiquated laws with regard to carriage of arms, thus adversely affecting their efficacy.

Taking a conceptual cue from the ministry of defence which has, in keeping with global practices, opened its resource pool to include the private sector, a public-private partnership could also be forged to tackle homeland security in India.

There are several reasons to do this.

Internal security in India is heading towards the perfect storm. In August, 2009 Indian security forces were planning to launch the largest ever offensive action against Naxalites. By sheer scale and spread, this operation will suck in several thousand government forces across scores of districts for the next three-four years.

Other environmental drivers such as intensification of the US operations in Pakistan and its fallout on infiltration of terrorists into India, resource deployment for Commonwealth Games, and deterioration of security situation because of sub-optimal monsoons will have the government resources stretched to their tethers.

Selective and structured privatization of the security value chain has been proven as an economic and efficient model in several countries. Most public installations, including airports, in developed countries are secured by private agencies under government oversight.

Australia outsources its prison and correction facilities. Israeli diplomats and even ministers are protected by private security firms. The US has farmed out entire chunks of the security value chain such as convoy protection, guarding of critical installations, maintaining lines of communications and the like even in war zones such as Iraq and Afghanistan.

In the Indian context, the public-private partnership has potential in several areas. For instance, training is one of the major challenges faced by the security forces. Training establishments are expensive to run and resource-hungry. They divert hundreds of officers and men who are desperately needed in operations into administrative roles.

The private sector could create world class training facilities, equip and man them, thus freeing the serving security forces from administrative and cost overheads.

Similar models have been used in the US to rapidly meet the demands of specialist skills required in urban warfare, counterterrorist operations, and intelligence gathering. The Israeli armed forces partner with private firms to train entire battalions and brigades.

This model also leverages the incredible pool of talent that is wasted away when servicemen retire with decades of operational experience behind them.

Consulting and project management is another domain where such partnerships can revolutionize efficiencies. Security establishments need expertise in areas of analytics, communication infrastructure, network centric warfare, and complex project management. Almost all of such work is outsourced to the private sector in developed nations. Given the nature of terrorism, much of such collaboration has to be in place in any case, because the terrorists use infrastructure such as telecom, Internet, public transportation, and financial networks to wage war against the state.

In the last decade, conflicts have undergone a paradigm shift. Battlefronts have moved from the borders into the cities, civilian assets are as vulnerable as military targets, and hostile states partner with non-state players to inflict damage on the economy—instead of capturing geographical territory.

It is also time for India to react to this shift and reorganize our resources from a traditionally government oriented format into a public-private coalition.

The key question is whether the government is ready for the mindset change required for a co-creative model and creating the environment for such participation.

— ◆ —

Citizen's Role in
Countering Terrorism

The logic that economic discontent breeds
the conditions for terrorism has manifested into the
belief that addressing poverty and economic
deprivation would lead to reduction of people
adopting the path of terror

It has been long believed that the root causes of terrorism lie in poverty, unequal growth, and lack of opportunity. Traditional wisdom seems to suggest that poor, discontented youth are the likeliest candidates for recruitment into the wrong side of the law. The logic flows something like this: All things remaining equal, poor neighbourhoods contain ingredients such as lack of educational facilities, lower quality of parenting, dearth of opportunity, exposure to violence, and disregard for the law.

The logic that economic discontent breeds the conditions for terrorism has manifested into the belief that addressing poverty and economic deprivation would lead to reduction of people adopting the path of terror. This view has had many proponents. Muhammad Yunus, in his Nobel Prize acceptance speech in 2006, said that it is essential to put resources into improving the lives of the poor to reduce the root cause of terror. There is a penchant to link terrorist movements all over the world to economic deprivation and lack of opportunity.

But facts indicate otherwise. On 7 July, 2005, four young men exploded bombs in three trains and a bus in London, injuring around 700 and killing 52. In March the previous year, Madrid was rocked by a series of blasts that were far more fatal, killing 191 and injuring 2,050 people. In both the cases, the perpetrators were not from poor backgrounds or lacking educational opportunities. One of the Madrid bombers owned a mobile telephone shop and the London bombers had university education.

Socio-economist Alan Krueger, in his Lionel Robbins Memorial lectures, argued that motivations for terrorism and crime are often confused with each other. The motivation for committing an act of crime is largely economic gain, but for blowing oneself up, a very likely outcome of a terrorist attack, is hardly an economic incentive. If poverty or illiteracy alone were to be the drivers for terrorism, then half the world's population that lives under $2 a day or 800 million illiterate adults would have torn the world apart with several terrorist acts every single day.

While some participants in acts of terror may be driven by financial incentives, these are usually naïve foot soldiers rather than senior or even middle-rung personnel. Empirical data has proved that although poverty has a strong correlation with crime, it doesn't influence terrorism. And, therefore, a strategy to combat terrorism needs to go beyond just economic measures. It needs to address some fundamental drivers that create and fuel terrorism.

The first driver—the core philosophy of terrorism—is also manifested in the terror act itself; the need to achieve an effect far greater than what the actual event warrants. The deaths of 166 people in the Mumbai attacks over three days pales in comparison with an estimated per day deaths caused by suicides (275), or traffic accidents (273). But suicides and traffic deaths don't get the publicity that terror attacks do. Terrorism 24×7 beaming live into the living room was a key factor during the Mumbai attacks. The driver is an attempt by a faction to exert an influence far beyond its legitimate numerical capability by spreading fear of violence beyond the immediate victims. The key word here is spreading.

The second driver is that terrorism is often economic greed cloaked in ideological causes. The start of the rainbow might have been ideological but the end of certainly has an element of material gain.

The third, and possibly the most deep-rooted driver, is angst at not being able to voice dissent by any other means. Terrorism is a tactic of politically motivated violence.

A national realization and commitment of its citizenry is essential to addressing these three drivers. When the anguished demands of a terrorized people start to influence the judgement of leaders, they are actually playing into the hands of the terrorists.

Terrorists and their criminal nexus use public and private infrastructure to conduct the preparatory aspects of their trade. All too often, most citizens diminish the need for their involvement or civic responsibility. Given the integrated nature of our social structures, these points of contact can serve as excellent early warning systems. Unfortunately, most inputs needed or sought by law enforcement are seen as a chore rather than an active contribution.

Addressing the third driver is possibly the best return on investment. The need to voice an opinion through violence is often preceded by several attempts at peaceful but ineffectual expressions. Legitimacy, unlike beauty, is seldom in the eye of the beholder. And it is truly ironic that we often learn of a new geography, its people and its problems, only when that place or issue has been put on the map with a stamp of terrorist violence.

Whether we like it or not, the world is one family and the problems of one region, country, or even continent are unlikely to remain confined to that place. To that extent, it is the responsibility of a nation's people to be cognizant of issues and viewpoints that could eventually find expression in violence, whether in their own nation or elsewhere. Because, ultimately, it does not matter if you are not interested in terrorism. Terrorism is definitely interested in you.

How the Public Can
Help Counter Terror

Unfortunately, set-piece battles are being rapidly replaced by irregular styles of waging war, where the frontlines are interspersed and civilians are as much in the combat zone as soldiers. In fact, in many conflicts civilians are no longer collateral damage—they are the intended target

For many of us who have been brought up learning about conflicts based on conventional wars, including the five that India has fought, the term 'being at war' connotes a formal announcement of hostilities, mobilization of forces, strident posturing, and military strikes, armies attacking on pre-determined thrust lines, capturing key towns and destroying assets. At some stage, the nuclear option would come into play. To avoid escalation, world powers would mediate and hopefully succeed. That is the set-piece sequence in a conventional war.

Unfortunately, set-piece battles are being rapidly replaced by irregular styles of waging war, where the frontlines are interspersed and civilians are as much in the combat zone as soldiers. In fact, in many conflicts, civilians are no longer collateral damage—they are the intended target. Also, conventional and irregular war, such as terrorism and insurgency, are not mutually exclusive. Often, a state uses both for improved leverage.

Ironically, this passive war is more insidious. Despite the devastation caused, conventional conflicts have a silver lining. All the wars that India has fought have been relatively short and localized and the general population was largely insulated from direct physical damage. Also, conventional war follows a predictable trajectory of build-up, preparatory strikes, a conflict stage, and an end.

Irregular instruments of hostilities, such as insurgency and terrorism, are far more menacing because of their very nature. Instigators of this format can select the ground of their own choosing, deep inside the state. The battle can be fought from within and outside with no clear demarcations between opposing forces.

The second feature of irregular wars is that they focus largely on civilian targets. Civilians are usually far more at risk than security forces, especially as they get caught in the crossfire of the state and the terrorists. Development suffers, opportunities dry up, and penury follows. Lack of alternatives fuels turbulence, and the vicious cycle goes on.

The very nature of terrorism puts security forces on the defensive, because terrorists can wrest the initiative more often. They can choose the time and place of the strike and vary the targets until security forces are spread thin or are exhausted. A clear lesson emerging is that the general population has to be co-opted in this battle against terror. They cannot remain neutral and uninvolved. Usually, this participation has translated into sporadic awareness campaigns that are not enough. To enable a paradigm shift, we need to attack the critical lynchpin that terrorist organizations need to thrive.

Societies make rules for governance and apparatuses for enforcing those rules. But many of these rules are not followed or are poorly enforced. One of the primary reasons of suboptimal execution of good intent is rampant corruption. It would be naïve to suggest that this bane will disappear soon. But perhaps the battle against terrorism offers an opportunity to address the issue and leverage an extraordinary force multiplier.

Think about it this way. While crime may or may not pay, society pays a heavy price for crime. For instance, the next time you see a broken-down truck clogging traffic on a busy road, appreciate the heavy price paid collectively in terms of time lost or fuel burnt—because some corrupt person certified the vehicle road-worthy. The amount he made as a bribe is minuscule compared with the cost the rest of society has to bear. Similarly, we spend far more to protect our houses from being burgled than the actual gains of all burglaries put together. These examples can be extrapolated to every instance when the resources used to prevent crime far exceed the actual benefit to the criminals.

Sociologists explain that this human behaviour of focusing on personal gain above that of the community is because the individual feels distanced from the effect of his misdemeanour. So the food adulterator believes that his family will not consume the adulterated food or the corrupt building contractor does not feel he will be affected by the bad construction.

However, terrorism is a game changer. The randomness and unpredictability of attacks removes the ability of a corrupt or even an indifferent facilitator to ensure that his loved ones will not be victims of his greed. In a way, terrorist strikes are great levellers. Because unlike many other crimes its victims range from commoners to rulers, from the poorest to the richest. In short, there is no rule to remaining safe, except that all of us follow all the rules.

Terrorists cannot operate in a vacuum. They need targets, transport, logistics, bases, finance, and communication. And because these components are leveraged from society, terrorists perforce have to rely on the apathy, indifference or outright corruption of various citizens to be able to operate.

So, convincing all stakeholders that their diligence has a direct bearing on the battle against terrorism is the vital step to wresting back the initiative in this battle. For instance, when the country addresses a debilitating problem like, say, population explosion or HIV, it carries out elaborate and sustained public awareness campaigns. Much in the same light, terrorism too needs to find its mindshare with public interest groups, non-governmental organizations, companies and, of course, the government, with sustained awareness campaigns at the grass-roots level to recruit active citizen participation. To enable true public participation in the battle against terrorism, citizens must realize that facilitating a terrorist act is like being an accessory—not a bystander.

The Boston Bombings and Aftershocks

India needs to relook its own hubris and national will to
address the terrorism menace before it gets too late

Over eleven years later, two explosions—suspected to be the
handiwork of terrorists—have rocked the US mainland again.
By any standard, this period of calm is an impressive record for
security agencies safeguarding the country. But they are also a
grim reminder that even a country with vast resources is not
immune from a terror strike in its territory. While the incident
itself is not significant in terms of damage and hardly holds a
candle to the previous one, it is a first of its sort and perhaps
may be a harbinger of worse to come.

While the Boston bombings may be puny compared with
some of the other recent attacks in other countries, they had
the potential to wreck far more havoc and clearly show that
terrorists' ambition and capability attacking the US mainland
are very much around. At a strategic level, security specialists
and administrators will be cringing at the renewed outlays
that will be diverted from an economy which is barely limping
back, bolstering the hawks who had been decrying the cuts.

The unexploded bombs found in vicinity of the athletic
event indicate a coordinated attack involving multiple explosions and, therefore, negate a 'lone gun' theory. The use
of ball bearings as explosive shrapnel and its placement at
ground level is a familiar ambush technique derived from military 'claymore' mines which is a lethal psychological weapon
because it results in many more amputees than deaths. The
former will serve as a grim reminder of this attack for the rest
of their lives. The choice of the legendary Boston Marathon
has the signs of professional siting because it is a high-profile
annual feature. One can read two things here. It would have
been a more difficult site to penetrate because of the inherent

security surrounding the event but would have ensured more live coverage of the blasts. The specific locations of the bomb near the finishing line with most number of cameras indicate this intent. Very clearly, this attack is a far more sophisticated one than the earlier Times Square one or the 'underwear' bomber.

All this leads to some disturbing suggestions. A coordinated attack, at the venue of a high-profile (and, therefore, high security) international event in a nation which has arguably invested immense resources—not just within the homeland but in several other countries—has succeeded. As of now it appears that neither was there any advance warning nor any immediate breakthroughs thus indicating a relatively higher degree of planning. Let us put this in context.

The US has one-sixth of India's population. It is straddled between two benign countries and two oceans. The US basically confronts threat of terror from primarily one or two entities. Almost all the country's records and information is captured in one language—English. Almost all residents in the US have a social security number and given the highly digital and largely legitimate economy, every transaction leaves a trail. The country and its cities are grid-locked with CCTV cameras of a wide variety and purposes. They have some of the most sophisticated and modern surveillance systems, which blend resources, technology, legislation, high political will, and public mindshare to address this threat. And they have been at it for the last 11 years.

Compare that with India, which has six times the US population; largely unmonitored, especially in the cities. Our records and information are maintained sketchily, inaccurately in several languages in mostly manual ledgers and registers. We are some distance away from a robust mechanism of linking transactions and people. A substantial part of our economy is not only cash-based but is also underground. And we are still struggling with IT modernization across the spectrum of public and large swathes of financial services. We face multiple threats from several hostile and unfriendly neighbours, internal dissidents, state-sponsored terror groups, criminals turned 'terrorists for hire' and, of course, evolved movements such as Naxalites and right-wing extremism. Our resource base is far lower and the implementation pace relatively slower.

Regardless of the perpetrator, the Boston attack is a wake-up call for the world. If terrorists can strike in a country that has the ability to carry its battle to any part of the planet with impunity, enforce its legislation on citizens of other countries, and is obsessed with security—then perhaps we need to relook our own hubris and national will to address this menace. And there is an irony here if we don't. The US and other countries of the world learnt and revamped their anti-terror strategies after the 26/11 attacks in Mumbai. Whether we realize the sense of urgency from the Boston bombings or not—we will certainly be paying the price for it, because every such event, starting with the Delhi Marathon later this year, will cost us far more than it did last year. The Indian exchequer will pay for the aftershocks of explosions half way across the world in perpetuity.

— ◈ —

Lessons Learned From
Armed Forces

Some Lessons on Participation from History Pages

War of any form needs a social context to be successful. It is not simply an assembly of more soldiers or a superior weapon that wins battles. Instead, it is the structured framework of a society that develops superior advantages

You would know from this book so far that I believe citizens need to play a greater role in securing our nation. We might think that citizens' participation is a sign of changing times, but history is replete with instances illustrating this concept. Here is one of my favourite stories.

In 1415, England's King Henry V invaded France and routed a French army of 30,000 with just 6,000 troops. The Battle of Agincourt (which lies between the port cities of Le Havre and Calais in the north of France) has gone down in history as one of the most startling and astonishing victories by a smaller force against a much larger one. This is a fascinating story of how an army that was weak and tired after months of battle inflicted a catastrophic defeat on an opponent five times its size in numbers and qualitative advantages.

And 600 years later, it still has lessons for us.

The English expeditionary force of 12,000 fresh and eager troops landed in France in August, 1415. They planned to capture the port town of Le Havre and move inland. But the siege lasted much longer than expected.

Attrition, dysentery, and skirmishes with the French depleted the English army to almost half the size before the garrison of Le Havre finally surrendered. Since the military campaigning season was coming to an end, Henry decided to move north to Calais. He realized that he did not have enough troops to wage a battle against the well-defended city of Rouen and yet could not return to England without losing face and the ability to sustain his campaign financially. Leaving a small contingent to guard Le Havre, Henry marched his weary army of just 6,000 soldiers north along the coast to Calais, hoping to draw the French out into battle.

On 25 October, he was met with the reinforced and invigorated French contingent of over 30,000 horsemen and foot soldiers in the epic battle of Agincourt. The battle itself lasted about five hours, at the end of which the French were annihilated with over 8,000 casualties against just 200 of the English.

The secret behind this extraordinary turn of the battle was the strategic advantage of the English longbow. The longbow, or the war bow as it was known then, was an awesome weapon. It was the height of a grown man and required great strength to draw to its full length. As a matter of fact, the draw weight or the pulling weight of the longbow was about 120 pounds, while the weight of the modern Olympic competition bow is 40 pounds.

Also, to unleash its full power, the arrow had to be pulled right behind the ear of the archer, thus offsetting the aim and making it inaccurate except in the hands of the most accomplished archers.

But what it gave in return was overwhelming power to the metal tipped arrow that could punch through the enemy armour. Some 5,000 English archers could fire 15 accurate arrows a minute each, unleashing a rain of 75,000 arrows every minute. This hail of steel shredded the attacking French waves into complete disarray and defeat.

The capability of the longbow ensured English superiority in almost all battles until well after the advent of the musket.

To be fair, the French had bows as well. They used the mechanically cranked crossbow, which fired a bolt further than the longbow, but the cranking process of reloading was much slower and the French archer could only manage about an arrow a minute. So why didn't the French use longbows as well? After all, it wasn't sophisticated technology that couldn't be copied. In fact, the French had imported expert bow makers from England to equip their own armouries as well.

The answer to this question illustrates why war of any form needs a social context to be successful. It is not simply an assembly of more soldiers or a superior weapon that wins battles. Instead, it is the structured framework of a society that develops superior advantages. While the longbow was a formidable weapon, its draw weight necessitated that the archer developed incredible power in his arms. To be a competent archer, he would have to start learning to shoot by the age of 10 or so and would need to practise 10-12 years before attaining proficiency. Skeletal remains of archers of the era confirm extraordinarily developed shoulders and arm muscles.

At the same time, kings could not afford to maintain large standing armies. They had to draw from the resources of lords and dukes or similar alliances whenever they went to battle. These archers had to work regular jobs when they were not fighting.

But the kings created this pool of archers by facilitating a passion for archery. They did this by offering prize monies and holding competitions at village, provincial, and central levels. Every village had a shooting range and kids 'played' archery during their spare time, in the hope of winning the prize money.

Soon it became a national pastime much like cricket did several hundred years later. Winners were honoured and given important positions in the armies, training and further incentives, thus creating an incredible and strategic advantage which gave the English superiority for centuries. That was an advantage that the French could not beat by technology alone. Though they tried to copy the English framework of disseminating training at the village levels, their social structure and the high cost of the crossbows made it impossible to replicate.

I think it is time for our society to realize that we cannot demarcate completely between soldiers and bystanders. War should remain the primary responsibility of soldiers, but the rest of the society too needs to participate.

While I am not an advocate of compulsory military training, I have a fair sense that if the government did offer it, there would be many takers. Of course, it will have to be made more convenient, and structures such as the National Cadet Corps, Territorial Army, and Civil Defence will have to be given the impetus and leadership that they need. It is important for our nation to start owning the responsibility of its security at all levels. A society that leaves its fighting to the soldiers and the thinking to the civilians risks creating soldiers who are dumb and civilians who are cowards.

— ◈ —

The Dilemma of Double Jeopardy

There are practical realities that must determine
whether the army should be called in to deal
with the Naxal issue

Lately there has been debate on the quantum and type of force
to be used in fighting Maoist insurgents. There is a strong lobby
that seems to be advocating employing the armed forces for the
job. To most outsiders, the army is an infallible organization that
takes on all tasks and delivers, unfailingly, every time. This track
record of reliability induces a temptation to use the army as a tool
for all situations. A temptation that has serious implications.

The reasons being cited for using (or not using) them seem
to be about protocol and role, among others. However, there
are practical realities that must determine whether the army
should be called in to deal with the Naxal issue. While there
are strategic and political implications to this step, facts merit
the bulk of the consideration.

What makes up the army and what are they trained for?
What are their core skills and are they equipped to cope with
the situation? Finally, are they the best suited for this? Let's
explore the answers to some of these questions.

The army's primary task is to protect the country from
external aggression. They have additional responsibilities such
as internal security and assistance to civil administration, but
their core responsibility is defending the nation.

And to do that, soldiers typically train nine months a year.
This training begins at the lowest level of a section of 10 men
right up to higher formations consisting of thousands of
soldiers. To take a raw recruit and convert him into a lethal killing machine requires hardening him physically and mentally,
training him in weapons and tactics and drilling him to operate in extreme circumstances with several other contingents.

A typical combat soldier trains and works for about 14 hours every day, 10 months in a year.

And then there is the training and maintenance of equipment. Soldiers of specialist battalions have to maintain fleets of armoured and fighting vehicles. They have to train to cross obstacles like raging rivers, cross complex bridging equipment, clear minefields and be able to do all this during day and night. They have to be ready to take on hostile aggressors across two fronts in the eventuality of war.

The rigour of this training is enough for any army man to take on any enemy, anywhere, anytime. To that extent, of course, the army could be deployed to address the Naxals in thick jungles and difficult, unknown terrains.

But are they the optimal choice?

The most important aspect of a soldier's training is his mental conditioning. That training is oriented towards a single-minded objective—destruction of the enemy. This ethos is imbibed in every element of training.

A visitor to any firing range of the Indian Army will find two edicts written on the walls: No mercy, no regret, no remorse, and ek goli, ek dushman (one bullet, one enemy). These aren't bravado graffiti. They are philosophical foundations on which the institution takes raw recruits from the mainstream community and converts them into fighting machines who will put their mission ahead of their own lives.

The first edict focuses on making the soldier impersonal and mission-focused. He has a task of capturing an objective and he will and must destroy anything that stands in the way—without mercy, remorse, or regret. And the second trains him for deadly efficiency. This is the reason why even in aid to civil authorities, the army never ever fires warning shots in the air. The first bullet the army fires is for effect.

The psyche of soldiers—which takes years to build—is what melds them into a fighting machine capable of achieving impossible odds. This is why their use for internal security must be considered in the light of three cautionary aspects.

One, internal security situations such as the Naxalite insurgency are a different ball game from all-out war. The emphasis is on minimum force, not overwhelming firepower. There are no enemies but citizens with different ideology who need to be integrated back into the mainstream.

And while there are hardcore elements within the Naxalites, the downside of collateral damage is very high. As the US Army has learnt at a great cost, very often its actions create the accidental guerrilla—someone who becomes a guerrilla because of collateral damage.

The second reason is that modern warfare calls for high degree of specialization. Each combatant has to train for several months in a year just to retain his fighting prowess. Distracting that soldier and unit comes at a high cost of their primary role, particularly for specialist units whose efficacy depends on continuity and integrated training.

Thirdly, if we deploy the army for internal roles, we will play into the hands of the adversaries whose strategy over the last 20 years has been to foment internal disturbance and tie down nearly half of the second largest army in the world. We would just reiterate that this strategy has great return on investment.

One of the fundamental principles of war is to focus the right resources for the right task. It is only prudent, therefore, that advocacy of army's employment for non-core tasks be considered in light of what dilution it would cause in their main role.

Else, we might end with a double jeopardy—the Naxal problem remains unresolved and an army that is believed to be infallible, fails—only because they were set up to do so.

— ◆ —

From Battlefields to Boardrooms

A planning framework used in military operations holds
lessons for improving corporate strategy and outcomes

In November, 2010, *Harvard Business Review* carried a cover
story on 'Leadership lessons from the military', focusing on
US war veterans returning from Iraq and Afghanistan, and
ways in which their field experience was being used in a
rapidly changing business environment. For a nation that has
realized the applicability of combat leadership (during three
distinct occasions—World War II, Vietnam war, and the Gulf
wars) in its corporate and political culture, this is not a new or
unknown phenomenon.

In fact, former military officers constitute just 3 percent of
the adult male population in the US, yet contribute three times
more to the CEO pool of S&P 500 companies. While the HBR
article makes for fascinating reading, I'm reminded of some
skills that the military teaches which can be used by anyone
regardless of what they do. These range from finding the north
using a watch (a neat trick to show your nephew, but not very
relevant in daily life) to developing a structured way of thinking.

These skills can be learnt in about half an hour and applied to
pretty much everything for a lifetime. This article explains one
of the best tools for structured thinking and communications.
It's a framework used by military commanders at all levels—
sergeants or generals—to develop plans and brief their teams.
Its design has been honed over thousands of years of combat
and through lessons learnt in blood. And it has stood the test
of time across different nations, situations, and domain areas.

A commander needs to think through various aspects
during planning. In complicated operations, missing elements
can be disastrous. To avoid this, the military uses a framework
informally named with the acronym 'Z-Kitbag.'

The leader starts by orienting his troops to the environmental landscape. 'Z' stands for 'zamini nishan'—landmarks in the theatre of operations. The commander first points out the north and the 'general line of direction'—a distant landmark used to centre the whole body of troops. This is critical because if the troops are dispersed on a broad front, then the two flanking extremes need to be aligned to one central line—else soldiers standing on the right and the left flanks will interpret directions differently.

Next, he explains the nature of the terrain, presence of roads, villages and resources, natural and man-made obstacles, and boundaries of adjoining formations. This ensures that every soldier is familiarized with the environment and its extents, and avoids trespassing on to sister formations.

In a business context, gaps in knowledge about zamini nishan cause leaders to take wrong decisions. Similarly, people who don't know their boundaries end up operating in areas which are not their domain. An incorrectly mapped individual can even turn out to be a hostile influence.

The next letter stands for 'khabar' or information. This part of the briefing always starts with khabar of the enemy: What their strength and disposition are; what kind of weapons they have, what resources they can call for from other theatres of operations; their commander and his traits—right down to the cultural behaviour of enemy troops. The second part of khabar deals with information about one's own troops and formations—friendly patrols that could be operating in the same area; capabilities and strengths; and most importantly, the location of one's own commanders.

The 'I' stands for 'irada,' or aim of the operation. This is a clearly defined objective that needs to be achieved within a certain time frame. The aim is repeated and rechecked from a few members by having them recite it verbatim—a practice that is sometimes forgotten in corporate communications.

'T' stands for 'tariqa,' or the strategy that will be adopted. It goes into details of where, when and how a mission will be accomplished: Who will be in charge of what part, and who will perform the role of a backup.

'Bandobast,' or resources and organization structure, comes next: What arrangements will be made for infiltration and extrication; where the rendezvous point is after the mission is accomplished; what the signal codes for success or failure will be; how reinforcements will be called for.

'A' stands for administration, or logistics: How much ammunition will be carried; how long the troops should prepare for; what the 'No-move-before' timing (the exact time until which the troops can be certain that they will not be called into operations) is.

And finally, 'G' stands for an important, yet often missed, aspect—'ghari milao,' or synchronization of all watches with the commander's watch. In military operations, a difference of even 20 seconds between the watches of assaulting units and artillery support can mean the difference between pummelled enemies or one's own troops caught in a barrage fired by supporting artillery. Translated into corporatespeak, this means aligning terms such as 'as soon as possible' or 'immediately' because these can imply different things to different people.

The sequence that the briefing follows also plays an important role. Each sub-unit commander knows which part of the sequence is relevant to him, and can, therefore, pay special attention when his portion begins.

This tool is several centuries old. For precisely that reason, it is but one of the many lessons that the corporate world can learn from the military.

— ◆ —

Keeping 'Certain Death' Alive

A daring rescue mission in war-torn Sierra Leone shows
the uses of combining different forms of intelligence

The significance of intelligence in any operation is undisputed.
However, debate rages over the importance of human versus
technical intelligence. Human intelligence, or Humint—as it
is known in tradecraft, is gathered using personnel deployed
on the ground—either by physical spying or running agents.
Technical intelligence, or Techint, is obtained through means
such as satellite imagery, photographic reconnaissance,
breaking ciphers and so on. Spy folklore and grassroots field
agents vaunt the value of Humint, while proponents of Techint
claim its superiority in the modern digital context.

However, as one of the most daring rescue missions ever
attempted demonstrates, intelligence is a formidable force
multiplier only when both techniques are used in conjunction.

In 2000, a team of the UK's Royal Irish regiment was
stationed in Sierra Leone to help train its armed forces. Sierra
Leone—a failed state for long—was in the throes of civil war,
with a multitude of rebel gangs ravaging the country. The most
feared of them was the 'Westside Boys' who controlled the
jungles outside the capital— Freetown. One particular outfit,
led by Foday Kallay, was notorious for its brutality. High on
drugs and alcohol, the outfit's standard modus operandi
comprised killing and torture, especially amputations.

On 25 August, 2000, a routine British patrol led by Maj.
Alan Marshall and accompanied by Sierra Leone liaison
officer Lt. Musa Bangura strayed into rebel-controlled jungles
and was ambushed by them. Facing overwhelming odds, Maj.
Marshall surrendered and tried to talk his way out. The Westside Boys had other plans. They whisked away the captives to
their stronghold of Geberi Bana, 50 km away. In the thick

jungles of Sierra Leone, that was as good as being in a different country. The hostages were brutally beaten and tortured, with Bangura being singled out for the worst treatment.

The next day, Kallay announced that he was holding the hostages and turned in his demands for amnesty, political recognition, and release of imprisoned comrades. The British realized the impossibility of meeting the demands and the need for a rescue operation. But they had no idea where to begin.

Over the next four days, Marshall and the other hostages came to the same conclusion—that they were fast running out of options. They knew it was only a matter of time before the volatile and crazed Kallay realized that the British wouldn't accede to his demands and started executing them. Marshall had to get information about where they were imprisoned to the rescue team. Using a scrap of paper and a pen, the hostages painstakingly drew a detailed map of Geberi Bana and their exact location in the hope that they would get an opportunity to communicate with the outside world.

On the fifth day of the crisis, that opportunity seemed to present itself. Col. Simon Fordham, the commanding officer of the Royal Irish battalion that the hostages were part of, met Kallay on the edges of the jungle to negotiate the terms of release. One of Kallay's demands was for a satellite phone, which would help him contact BBC and internationalize the situation. In return, he promised to release five hostages. Kallay had brought with him a battered Marshall and his second-in-command Capt. Flaherty as 'proof of life.' As Flaherty and Marshall shook hands with their commanding officer, they managed to pass him the map of the stronghold. At last, the British knew exactly where the hostages were being held and the disposition of rebels in the area.

Now the British high command had to make a difficult decision. While it had begun negotiations with Kallay to buy time, the ministry of defence had realized that any rescue mission more than 3,000 miles into hostile territory was suicidal. However, 70 commandos from the British Special Air Service and Special Boat Service as well as 100 soldiers of the Parachute Regiment (nicknamed Paras) were ordered to embark on Operation Barras. This was to be the deadliest rescue mission ever attempted since World War II. Aptly, the unofficial codename was 'Certain Death'.

Now that they knew where to begin, Britain deployed its Techint capability along the Rokel river, where the hostages were being held. Satellites mapped the terrain to develop rescue strategies. The commandos were faced with a danger-ous conundrum. Their plan must get them to the rebels before the rebels could get to the hostages. Given the latter's proxim-ity to the hostages, the commandos would have only seconds before the kidnappers executed all of them.

The combination of Humint and Techint helped build a detailed picture of the operational area. It was a grave one. Kallay and 150 rebels held the hostages in a stronghold in the middle of dense forest on the northern bank of the Rokel. There were another 100 rebels armed with heavy weapons on the opposite bank in the village of Magbeni. Additionally, there was absolutely no way for the commandos to reach the stronghold by road without losing the element of surprise. The river option was also abandoned when a reconnaissance team realized that hidden sandbags had been placed to prevent a river-borne approach. With such hurdles, the mission was already in danger of failure.

— ◆ —

Keeping 'Certain Death' Alive—II

How intelligence helped a rescue mission on the brink of failure to become the turning point in a gruesome civil war

As Operation Barras took shape in the dense jungles of Sierra Leone, an observation team of Britain's Special Air Service (SAS) was inserted on foot within 250 metres of the rebel camp where British soldiers were being held captive by rebel leader Foday Kallay. Armed with specialized equipment, the team had a ringside view of the camp and the serious condition of the hostages. First-hand observation about the number of rebels, their weapons and morale allowed the British to develop the final assault plans.

The close proximity of the other rebel camp across the Rokel river meant that the two would have to be neutralized simultaneously. On the 17th day of the crisis, then Prime Minister Tony Blair gave the go-ahead, and six helicopters took off using the most dangerous approach to any rescue mission. An airborne assault has two major disadvantages. First, the noise of the helicopters gives away the element of surprise well before the commandos can slither down into the firefight. Second, helicopters are sitting ducks while they hover to disgorge the commandos.

In 1993, US Special Forces had attempted a similar mission in Mogadishu into the stronghold of Somalian warlord Farrah Aidid. But two of their Black Hawk helicopters had been brought down; the raid had resulted in 18 deaths; and instead of surgical 30-minute operation, troops had been pinned down in enemy territory for 17 hours.

The US raid had heavy armoured ground support, which had finally extricated the beleaguered airborne troops. The British were going to attempt their operation without any such backing. If they failed, over 150 soldiers would be slaughtered in the jungles.

At dawn on 26 September, 2000, two attack teams in three Chinook helicopters approached Geberi Bana and Magbeni simultaneously. The SAS commandos would attack Kallay's camp to rescue the hostages, and elements of the Parachute Regiment (Paras) would suppress the rebel group at Magbeni to prevent them from bringing their heavy weapons into play. Three Lynx helicopters accompanied the Chinooks providing close air support.

Fortunately, the rebels at Geberi Bana were nursing a hangover from a binge the previous night. This had been one of the intelligence inputs provided by the SAS observation team. Though the helicopters skimmed the treetops to minimize the noise, the rebels heard the thump of the rotors before the choppers reached their designated landing zones and started organizing themselves. But within moments the Chinooks reached their designated holding pattern and laid down heavy suppressive fire.

Roused from his sleep, Kallay shouted orders to execute the hostages. A few rebels began running towards the hut where the hostages cringed in fear. The rescue team designated to extricate them had not yet reached, and it seemed that the hostages would be killed before it could. The mission could turn into a complete disaster.

Fortunately for the hostages, there was a third element in play. After a week of watching from the periphery, marksmen from the SAS observation team had inched forward and were placed between the rebels and the hostages. Their precision fire cut down the rebels while the extrication team secured the hostages. The commandos then began searching for the liaison officer who had been kept in a separate hut.

111

Meanwhile, the assault in Magbeni was running into major problems. A chance mortar explosion had wounded many Paras officers and the rebels were regrouping with heavy weapons. Capt. Danny Matthews of the Paras took over command and called for air support. As the Lynx laid down strafing fire, the Paras charged the rebels and annihilated the Magbeni camp.

Within 30 minutes it was all over. The rescue team lifted out of the battle zone with all the prisoners and their own injured (one of them, fatally). They also had a bonus cargo on board. Foday Kallay had been captured alive hiding under his bed.

This operation was a turning point in Sierra Leone's history. The fearsome reputation of British commandos swept through other camps, where rebels dreaded that they would be the next to wake up to the thump of helicopters. Many began surrendering. Within months, the rebels were routed.

Operation Barras has many lessons, least of which is the combined potential of technical and human intelligence. The operation could not have got off the drawing board without the scrap of paper that gave planners the first break; it could not have succeeded without the information obtained through satellite imagery. The minute by minute intelligence fed by the SAS observation team on the ground, and their intervention at critical moments, were the pivots on which the operation hinged.

A third critical element was the political decisiveness and resolute action by Blair in authorizing what is now acknowledged to be one of the most risky rescue missions of all time. But the results were worth it. All hostages were rescued intact for the loss of one commando. The psychological impact went further—it became the hinge around which the Sierra Leone government could seize the initiative back from the rebel militia.

And Foday Kallay was sentenced to 50 years in prison.

— ◆ —

The 70 Years to Abbottabad

Unconventional tools such as the SEALs who took out
Osama have changed the face of the war on terror

A key component of the US raid on Abbottabad had its
origins in a military operation over 70 years ago in the island
of Tarawa, which Japan had occupied during World War II.
This was one of the first American offensives in the Pacific
region, and possibly the toughest. Of the 35,000 US marines
who landed in Tarawa on 20 November, 1942, over 6,000 died
in just the three days of fighting it took to claim the island.
One of the major reasons was that the assaulting units had
no knowledge of underwater corals and obstacles, where
hundreds of marines perished without firing a single shot.

This tragic incident triggered the creation of a unit that was
capable of operating underwater in enemy-controlled territory. Specially trained commandos handpicked from within the
US Navy were trained in underwater demolitions and deep-sea
incursions. They could then be launched from floating crafts
and submarines. Since the enemy would still be able to pick
out the radar signature of the launch platform, in later years
this elite team was trained to execute airborne insertions using
the HALO, or 'High Altitude, Low Opening,' format of parachute jumps. This allowed commandoes to be dropped directly
off the shoreline from very high altitude aircraft—which could
pose as commercial airliners—along with specialist equipment
such as raiding crafts or submerged breathing apparatus. A
later variant that enabled parachuting at high altitudes allowed
commandos to 'fly' several hundred kilometres on their own
after jumping from the aircraft.

With this three-dimensional capability, the team was
deemed capable of operating in sea, air and land, giving it the
name SEAL. SEAL team commandos led the American thrust

on developing capability in unconventional warfare. By the 1960s, they had started working with the Central Intelligence Agency's (CIA) highly secretive Special Actions Division and later the Studies and Operations Group (SOG) in Vietnam. SOG's mission was to carry out an intensified programme that comprised harassment, sabotage, capturing prisoners, causing diversion of resources, physical destruction, and propaganda. Later, this lethal combination—CIA espionage and political engineering expertise, along with the surgical strike capability of the Special Forces—was ported to different theatres of war such as Korea, Iraq, Afghanistan, and now Pakistan.

While the SEALs were 'limelighted' in the 2 May mission, they are as the trade calls them—the 'sharp end of the stick' which needs to be backed by formidable resources. Raid and rescue missions are extremely complex by nature. The intelligence is never conclusive; there is always some ignorance about local target conditions, which are usually well protected; and it almost always involves working with other actors. In addition, several variables come into play. A small technical malfunction, which would be just a hiccup in regular operations, can start a chain of disastrous events in raids —as was the case in the infamous Tehran embassy rescue attempt in 1980.

While the SEALs have had their share of glory and setbacks, the US has continued to invest heavily in nurturing its special forces. More importantly, it has cultivated extensive experience of using them in irregular warfare—a hard-earned but force-multiplying skill.

Four aspects are critical in any systematic response to proponents of terror, be they state or non-state players, or both. These are: the conventional armed forces, diplomatic and economic efforts, the intelligence apparatus and finally, Special Forces and other tools of unconventional warfare.

The modern trend is one of conventional forces providing the anvil or umbrella cordon for operations. Diplomatic and economic efforts undermine the terrorists' resolve and deny wherewithal to the enemy. But in the war against terror, the real game changers are intelligence-based, strategic high-value operations conducted by Special Forces, followed up by propaganda and psychological operations. Missions planned and led by the CIA, and executed by small groups of specialist military commandos, are fast becoming the favoured format to disrupt terrorist networks whose leaders now fear that the next raid might be coming for them.

With the Abbottabad operation, the US has reiterated that 'hot pursuit' as an instrument of war has incredible strategic returns on investment. The 38-minute operation required painstaking preparation over four years, led by the CIA and assisted by a number of other agencies, including the National Security Agency, the National Geospatial-Intelligence Agency, and the department of defence. The intelligence was collected using unmanned drones as well as 'feet on the ground' by CIA-operated surveillance teams around Osama bin Laden's hideout, and tens of millions of dollars were sanctioned for this operation alone.

It must be conceded that in the world of Special Forces operations, successful missions are lesser known than failures that are highlighted. But with this raid, the US has joined the elite club of countries that are reputed for taking the battle personally to top terrorist leaders, and hunting them down rather than waiting for the next attack to happen.

The Primitive Origins of War

War is a planned and coordinated manner of robbery
that originated some 10,000 years ago

Despite all the achievements of mankind, as a species we
present a paradox to future generations. One could question
why humans—unarguably the 'smartest' animal to inhabit
the planet—would devote so many resources to destroying
their own kind. Man is the only animal to have changed the
environment to his needs, rather than just adapting to the
constraints imposed by it. It is also the only animal to grasp the
concept of delayed gratification: the concept of sacrificing now
for greater benefit in the future. Then why do we consistently
destroy our own environment, pollute the air we breathe, or
the water we drink? Why does the brain, which can envision
projects yielding results after decades, commit actions that
lead to disasters in a matter of months? Why is man the only
animal that commits atrocities such as genocide on others of
its own species or ecocide on his own environment?

The easy answer of course would be self-centred emotions
such as greed, selfishness, etc., but these are behaviours at an
individual level. And while individual or occasional acts of self-
destruction can be put down to personality or circumstances, a
series of such acts by an entire species suggest a hardwiring of
destructive behaviour that can push us over the abyss, unless
we understand and correct it.

Conflict is as old as our species itself. Mankind, as we know it,
evolved physiologically about four million years ago. However,
our species' cultural evolution happened less than 200,000
years ago. During this comparatively short period, man learnt
his most important survival skill—the ability to work in groups.
Ironically, anthropologists suggest the development of this

core skill that differentiates mankind—our ability to plan and communicate—stemmed from 'war'.

Early man foraged for food before evolving into farming and hunting. While farming was fraught with uncertainties such as weather, water supply and the delays between sowing and harvesting, hunting was immediate, and man was able to supplement his food with instant protein in the form of meat. But hunting posed its own challenges. Man quickly learnt that it was better to hunt groups of large animals so that more meat could be obtained from each hunt. Also large animals like the mammoth meant more fat, fur, and bones. The first two were essential to survive the cold and the bones helped make tools.

But this action of a communal hunt gave mankind more than just food or clothing. When prehistoric men banded together to track, stalk and bring down a large animal, they needed to accomplish the sophisticated task of planning and organizing a hunt, which is warfare in primitive form. They needed to communicate a complex set of instructions with precision (later to be known as military precision) to individuals who may not even be a part of their band. These individuals would have to work in smaller sub-units under junior leaders. Elements of an organization, leadership under stress, terse unambiguous orders, and situational shift in headship were all born out of the need to fight together to take on a larger 'enemy'. Hunting became the seed for many powerful frameworks that distinguish our species—such as collaborative strategies, social structures, situational leadership, and communication.

As man evolved, the basic unit of a 'family' enlarged to kinsmen, then clans, tribes, and eventually nations. It was a matter of survival that the clans and tribes were 'right-sized'. They had to be large enough to provide enough manpower for the communities' needs and yet not have too many mouths to feed. So when the size of the tribe grew beyond what the lay of the land could sustain, clans would move or hive off on adaptation paths of their own.

Mankind's secret to survival and becoming the most proliferate species on earth was not being the fittest. As anthropologist Jacob Bronwski points out, environment exacts a price from the fittest. It imprisons them within the confines of that environment. For mankind to proliferate, it had to adapt to the freezing cold of the Arctic and to the searing heat of the deserts. Also being an animal that had no integral weapons (such as claws and teeth to hunt) or bodily defence mechanisms (such as fur or armour), humans had to adapt and create survival strategies—the first of which was the act of war.

We often confuse fighting or conflict with war. Fighting is a much baser instinct hardwired in our primordial brain. A dangerous situation produces the same physiological reaction in us today as it did millions of years ago in our ancestors.

So whether faced with a tiger or a mugger—the adrenalin rush, suspension of digestive activities, twitching of muscles, nervous palpitation, etc., are all responses of the body getting ready to fight or flee. Conflict is a mental and physical state where two different instincts are chosen depending on the situation. These are instincts that drive a predator to hunt its quarry or help female mammals protect their young. War, on the other hand, is a planned and coordinated form of theft that originated about 10,000 years ago.

Demons and Angels

Humans can inflict terrible cruelty or be incredibly selfless—society needs to choose the right role model

In 1961, Yale University psychologist Stanley Milgram sought to answer a question that had perturbed the civilized world for decades. He wanted to know how thousands of soldiers and civilians in Nazi Germany could participate in the extermination of millions of Jews and other 'undesirable' people. How was it possible that perfectly normal people would commit acts that go against the moral conscience and values of human civilization? Could a holocaust happen again in any country or environment—or were Hitler and Nazi atrocities an aberration of normal human behaviour?

The Milgram experiment cast subjects into the role of 'tutors' who were supposed to teach their 'students' a list of words and were directed to punish them for wrong answers. The punishment was in the form of increasing voltage of electricity administered to the student at the press of a button by the 'tutor'. The range increased from a mild 15 volts shock incrementally to a dangerous 300 volts to a fatal 450 volts.

Unknown to the subject, an actor played the part of the 'student', and was located in another room, but within earshot so that the 'tutor' could hear simulated screams of the student. Before the experiment, Milgram polled several psychologists to get their sense of how many 'tutors' would administer painful shocks and the answers were consistent with normal belief that only a small minority—fewer than 1 percent—would have sadistic tendencies. However, when the experiment got under way (and Milgram did 16 separate studies), the startling results were that more than two-thirds of the thousand subjects he tested administered the fatal level of 450 volts.

Many subjects were traumatized during the experiment, but once reassured that they were not personally responsible for damage caused to the 'student' and the experiment was being done for a 'larger' purpose, over 60 percent of the subjects went on to perform what was clearly an atrocity on another human who had done them no harm. Variants of Milgram's experiment have been performed in several countries—more famous among them being the Stanford Prison experiment conducted at that university—all of which reiterate that humans are capable of incredible levels of evil if certain conditions are met. The belief that only a small percentage of us are capable of sadistic behaviour is factually incorrect.

Psychologists attribute this deviation from one's personal code of conscience to 'deindividuation' or transfer of personal responsibility onto the group. Philip Zimbardo, the conductor of the Stanford experiment, identified specific social processes that lead down the slippery slope of moral decay, which begins with taking the first step of administering 15 volts rationalized by 'it is so mild that the student can hardly feel it'!

This is precipitated by the dehumanizing of others, abdication of personal responsibilities, uncritical conformance to the group, and passive tolerance by inaction or indifference.

The implication of such behaviour is chilling. Our children and future generations are exposed to far higher degrees of violence in games, TV, movies and world events, inuring them to the first step of using violence as an acceptable way of quashing dissent. Critical views are marginalized and societies are exhibiting indifference and inaction as responses to social issues. This is a bigger challenge for India because of its diversity and expanse where major problems seem distant and unconnected. The behaviour of lynch mobs and violent instances of road rage or hate crimes expose the deterioration of our much-lauded tolerance. Every generation sets the benchmark of behaviour for the next and if current trends are anything to go by—we are setting a dangerous role model.

But the good news is that the behaviour of societies can also be influenced positively by selfless exemplars who put the well-being of others ahead of their own. In July 2007, a young student, Cameron Hollopeter, fell in front of an incoming train at a subway station in Manhattan. With the speeding train literally metres away, death seemed certain, but for the actions of a 50-year-old black American, Wesley Autrey. He jumped onto the track and, realizing that he would not be able pull Hollopeter out of harm's way, performed an act of selfless bravery for a complete stranger, while his own two small daughters stood watching. Autrey pushed the student down flat in between the tracks and lay on top of him, allowing the train to pass over both of them with an inch of clearance. When asked later, Autrey said that he did what anyone could do—and everyone ought to do.

Closer home, we have several instances of brave hearts who decided not to be bystanders, though they could have and remained alive.

Employees of the Taj who went back into the hotel during the terror attack to assist guests, or the nurses who died saving patients in the hospital blaze in Kolkata, bear testimony to the inherent heroism and nobility in all of us.

Philip Zimbardo chronicled the Stanford experiment in his book 'The Lucifer Effect' and, ominously enough, the behaviour exhibited by his students was replicated three decades later in the prisons of Abu Ghraib by the US army—though the latter chose to explain it away as deviant conduct by a few individuals. It is, therefore, important to recognize that our behaviour is shaped by social forces that can bring out the demons or angels existing within each of us. And it is the collective responsibility of society as to which of these two avatars becomes the archetype for future generations.

Surviving a Perfect Storm

Business companies have a lot to learn from the military when it comes to understanding uncertain environments

'No plan survives first contact with the enemy'—Carl Von Clausewitz's aphorism—seems prophetic in current volatile times. Businesses, governments, and individuals are facing uncertainties battling variables they don't control and scenarios they cannot possibly envision. Long-term plans seem fairy tales when goal posts shift every quarter. How can leaders plan or deliver their mandates in this 'fog of uncertainty'?

An approach perhaps lies in learning how successful military leaders deliver in environments where 'fog' is pretty much the operating system. Yet military plans need exactness because any imprecision can result in catastrophe. Successful military leaders have resolved this paradox in an interesting manner.

To begin with, a good commander thoroughly familiarizes his junior leaders with the campaign's overall intents and his 'general line of direction' even while specific plans are being sketchily developed and percolated down to the last man. This allows officers to know the extent of leeway they have when situation is not going according to plans and they can assume orders when communications break down—a very frequent occurrence during combat. Success (or failure) is measured in ranges, rather than absolutely precise metrics. Good commanders realize that on-ground leaders best know a fluid situation and, hence, while adequate diligence may be exercised in selection of the leader, once he has been given command, he gets considerable freedom—within the predetermined range.

The education frameworks of most business schools still instill an expectation of precision. Numbers are sacrosanct and an inability to meet targets reflects poorly on the leader. While this philosophy may serve well during relatively stable times, they are doomed to fail during volatile periods. When unforeseeable events half way across the world can change the business environment overnight, expecting business leaders to deliver on annually approved plans is hoping for a miracle. Different measurements are needed in turbulent times.

One way is to start defining success as furthering the general intent of stakeholders. In business, this happens to be profitability. Instead of holding business leaders accountable to absolute targets of top and bottom line, boards ought to look at ratios instead. The measurement criteria must encourage leadership to realign their resources and stay on a par with the ratios between the top and bottom line instead of demanding adherence to year-old targets as the latter is clearly unrealistic.

However, under existing paradigms, CEOs and business heads view downgrading of absolute targets as a sign of failure and, are therefore, averse to do so until reality forces them to. This reluctance also introduces a tendency of 'optimistic lying' and senior management is often not told the harsh truth.

Second, turbulent times need rapid iterations of environmental scans. Before the start of any military campaign, planning data is relatively static. Ground conditions, enemy troop strength, terrain, weather, etc., are elements that don't change greatly. However, once operations start, operational maps are constantly updated allowing commanders to view the changing situation in near real time. This requires increased recce elements on ground and a philosophy that it is 'okay' to change.

Business plans, too, are developed based on market opportunities and other environmental variables. But if these are not constantly updated and revised, then any plan based on the older version is actually worse than no plan at all. This means more frequent communication with front-line leaders with an intent to learn, not chastise. It also means allowing them a greater leeway in grabbing fleeting opportunities as and when they appear. Instead, during volatile periods many managements practise the reverse by tightening control and dampening local initiative.

Most organizations are flexible while planning and rigid during execution. However, that construct may not serve well during fluid situations. The D-Day landings in Normandy during World War II took years to plan. Millions of men, equipment, resources and hundreds of operations had to be synchronized to deliver the largest armada known to man, against estimated (but uncertain) enemy opposition. However, the allied commanders knew that once they contacted German defence, any form of close coupling of intricate plans could jeopardize the entire operation. So, they used an ingenious mixture of philosophies. Individual soldier-level drills were rehearsed repeatedly and perfected like clockwork. Subunits practised together so that various components of the invading force could work in synchronization with other units.

However, operational plans were left to dynamic front-line leaders who could group and regroup subunits and even make high-ranking changes in command. So, while subunit commanders were led on a tight leash during the invasion, they were given a freer hand once they made contact with enemy. The overall allied operational schedule went astray by months, but victory was certain.

Contrastingly, while Hitler had the best operational general in Rommel with him at Normandy, he chose to retain personal control over the strategic Panzer divisions refusing to release them to Rommel until it was too late. This stance contributed to German defeat more than anything else during the D-Day landings.

Companies, especially larger conglomerates, must realize that during volatile times, it is the front-line leaders who are best qualified to make operational changes and decisions. They need more resources at their local control while senior management needs to hold their nerve and trust the judgement of the former. It is their job to make more resources available to them and give less advice.

Finally, turbulent times are when the mettle of leadership is truly tested. Anyone can be a successful leader during good times just like any port is safe for a ship during a storm, but that is not what ships (or leaders) are made for.

India's Quest for the Top Gun

Selecting the right fighter jet often involves reconciling
contradictory technical needs with strategic doctrine

With announcement of Rafale as the Indian Air Force's (IAF)
next generation fighter, the dogfight among six of the world's
leading aircraft seems to have ended. However, those unfamil-
iar with weaponization strategies might wonder how countries
decide upon any weapon system. Is it simply a matter of the
best? If so, what is best?

The answer isn't straightforward. The choice of a weapon
system has less to do with specifics of its technical capabilities and more with imperatives of strategic doctrine. To understand this better, let's start the journey from a lowly assault rifle
rather than a sophisticated aerial platform such as a fighter jet.

An assault rifle is the mainstay of infantry, i.e. bulk of the
fighting force of any country, and has over 10 design parameters which are often contradictory. For instance, a rifle should
be accurate, have long range, be easy to maintain, sturdy
enough to survive the rigours of battlefield, have a rapid rate
of fire, and easy to handle with one hand for urban combat.
In addition, the weapon must be light, have compact ammunition of the same calibre as other weapons so that supply chain
logistics are manageable. It must have the capability to be used
in different versions, for instance, paratroopers need shorter
rifles and infantry support groups need longer ranges. Each of
these requirements contradicts many others.

For example, accuracy over long ranges means the barrel will
have to be long and the rate of fire cannot be high. This in
turn makes the rifle unwieldy and suboptimal in a fierce firefight. If the rifle has to be sturdy with heavy munitions then
it can't be light and soldiers will tire before they enter battle.

Such complications exacerbate as weapon platforms get

more complex. For instance, let's consider the battle tank. The North Atlantic Treaty Organization (Nato) designers were compelled to build heavier tanks because their theatres are limited in space and their tanks had to be heavily armoured to hold ground without ceding position. A lesson reinforced by the German blitzkrieg when France was overrun in a matter of days. Also, Nato countries have comparatively low manpower though they are better skilled and educated. Hence, tanks such as the British Chieftain and French Leclerc were designed upward of 55 tonnes, have high crew comfort, and the crew is 'dual traded', i.e. each member of the crew is expected to know more than just his own job, necessitating higher investments in training and retention.

The Soviets, however, relied on a much lighter and cheaper tank of the T54/55 series, because they could trade 'time for space'. The Soviet strategy was to let invaders enter deep into the Russian hinterland—a situation they could afford, primarily because of their strategic depth—and then hit the supply chains through encirclement and, of course, the assistance of 'General' Winter. The 'Warsaw doctrine', therefore, catered to Russia's strengths which are plentiful supply of conscripted manpower, manoeuvring space and the severe weather where sophisticated equipment had more chances of failure. These strategies are consistent with their assault rifles as well. While the West has relied on relatively sophisticated weapons such as the American M16, British FAL and the French Famas, the Soviets developed the cheap but reliable AK-47 series.

The key to understanding these strategies is to appreciate that in combat, a weapon is never pitted against another weapon in purely technical terms. It is, instead, a combination of the technical prowess, soldier's capabilities, terrain, and the national doctrine which decides the optimum arraignment of weapon platforms. So, while a sophisticated Heckler and Koch rifle could be an ideal weapon for highly-trained special forces, a much cheaper and rugged AK-47 is better suited for mass infantry attacks, though on a purely technical comparison, the Heckler would outgun the AK.

Fighter aircraft are sophisticated weapon platforms and, hence, their inter-linkage is far more complicated. Modern fighters are expected to perform 'omniroles'. They have to be highly manoeuvrable for 'air-to-air' dogfights, possess heavy lift capability for tactical and strategic bombing, have long radius of action, be capable of operations from land and sea, etc. Their supply chain is even more complicated, especially for India, which has a wide and diverse area of geographical interest. Fighters need air refuelling, naval carriers, multi-weapon capability, an intricate web of radars, airborne warning and control system, sophisticated maintenance, repair and overhaul facilities, and indigenous manufacturing to minimize external dependence.

They also need synchronization with other arms such as the army and navy. For, while IAF may pummel the enemy and establish air superiority, it is of little use unless armoured formations can rapidly exploit this hole and pour into enemy territory. And the latter's ability to do that is contingent on their own modernization programme which depends on the country's threat perceptions and mitigation strategy over the coming decades.

Viewed from this perspective, it is rarely the technical supe-riority of any single weapon system that matters. Instead, it is the complex 'organization for battle' derived from strategic doctrine which serves as credible deterrence. And deterrence is what it must be—because as any soldier will affirm, war is an ironic game. The only winning move—is not to play.

— ◈ —

Conflicts and Inventiveness

From weapons design to development of tactics, human resourcefulness comes to the fore in perilous times

A fascinating aspect about conflict is the human resourceful-
ness during such perilous times. This ingenuity manifests itself
in weapons design, development of tactics, and even demonstration of the leadership's confidence in their soldiers. Interestingly, each country displays its inventiveness in a manner
unique to its own culture and strengths.

For instance, during World War II, Germany, which had
an excellent engineering legacy, inducted a wide range of
weapons, including the Luger pistol for the elite Waffen SS.
This beautiful piece of weaponry was handcrafted and is still
considered an all-time classic blend of precision, accuracy,
and sophistication. So much so, that the Luger became the
most sought after souvenir by allied troops advancing through
Western Europe and the Germans were so possessive of this
iconic weapon that they would unhesitatingly shoot anyone
found with a Luger—a punishment normally reserved only for
spies and saboteurs.

For all its virtues, the Luger had one fatal failing. Its precision
engineering caused dust and grime to jam the pistol during the
time it was needed the most. Many a German soldier discovered this to his peril during a fierce firefight. The German
engineers, however, believed that they had a perfect design
in the weapon itself; evidenced by the fact that the precision
obsessive Swiss army had also chosen the Luger as its standard
sidearm. The solution they came up with was in the form of
an exquisite leather holster which covered the pistol in a snug
tight fit, thus preventing dust and grime from getting to it.

The Russians on the other hand had to develop a weapon that
would offset their weakness while leveraging their strengths.

Most of their troops were young uneducated farmhands who would need to fight in extreme weather and terrain conditions. They lacked the training to care for sophisticated weapons and in any case, the Russian manufacturing process favoured mass produced simple but effective, zero maintenance firearms. So they took a German sub-machine gun design and adapted it to produce the ubiquitous and iconic assault rifle that would go on to see more service than any modern weapon ever produced by man—the AK-47. While the AK-47—and its modern variant the AK-74—is a very effective assault rifle in all respects, its forte is unflinching reliability. The AK has been known to operate effectively despite any possible abuse that man or nature could throw at it. A fact that has resulted in more than a hundred million of them being produced and despite its lack of sophistication this weapon has found its way into the armies of several countries other than Russia—including India.

Sometimes, tactics need to be modified to suit new circumstances. The British Special Air Service (SAS), which is the forerunner of many anti-terror outfits in the world, had its roots in the deserts of Libya where they operated in jeeps deep inside enemy territory destroying enemy aircraft. For this they had six heavy machine guns per jeep which were capable of spewing awesome firepower on the enemy. Though the SAS was disbanded after World War II and re-raised in many avatars, the massacre of Israeli athletes in Munich in 1972 prompted its resurrection as one of the finest anti-terror commando units ever to see service.

From the legacy of long range high-powered guns, SAS now had to adopt low velocity weapons which are necessary for hostage rescue situations. A high-powered bullet would simply go through the intended target and hit several hostages in the line of fire. However, the Browning pistol that the SAS used during its nascent stages had a problem. Its 9mm, low velocity round had relatively less stopping power. The terrorist could still fight even after he was shot. Rather than increasing the velocity and thus endangering innocent hostages, the SAS created the famous 'double tap' or two shots fired in quick succession onto the chest or head—a practice which has permeated into every special force of the world; as Osama bin Laden discovered in May, 2011 when he was taken down by the SEALs with a chest and head shot.

But perhaps the most remarkable of all stories in this genre, is the one about the SAS 'killing house'. This two-floor facility was created to train commandos in high-risk hostage rescue situations where they have to storm a building in darkness amid smoke and confusion to kill the perpetrators without hurting the hostages. And all this has to be achieved within seconds to prevent hostages being killed by their captors. Significantly, commandoes train using live ammunition in the killing house as they believe that all exercises must be realistic, notwithstanding the frequent risk of fatalities.

But what is truly incredible is that the 'killing house' has had many dignitaries as visitors, including the royal family and Prime Minister Margaret Thatcher who chose to sit in the position of a hostage during one such demonstration. Seconds later, SAS commandoes exploded stun grenades and stormed into the room shooting targets inches from her head—using live ammunition and successfully 'extricated' her. The Iron Lady, who had ordered the SAS into the Iranian embassy in May 1980, showed the faith she reposed in their abilities in the most unequivocal manner possible.

Understanding National Defence and Our Role

The Indian Armed Forces are responsible for guarding a border across traditional and nuclear enemy nations; hostile and/or disturbed nations and disputed areas like Jammu and Kashmir

If the average Indian was asked to name one organization that continues to do the nation proud after about 62 years of independence, the answer would probably be the Armed Forces. This institution has remained secular, apolitical, insular, and superbly efficient; unlike the general deterioration of virtually every other establishment of the same vintage. Be it in their primary role of defending against external aggression from five fronts, handling internal security duties in different regions or helping civilians during natural or man-made disasters, the Armed Forces have conducted themselves exemplarily each time they have been called to action. This track record is reflected even in global theatres where the Forces have won admiration and accolades for the country.

Despite their incredible role in nation building, the Armed Forces have remained an enigmatic organization to most people. Most nations teach their population about their army, the history of eventful battles, organizational structures, and some basics of civil defence. Bookstores across the world are stocked with volumes on military history and operations. Yet, even educated Indians would probably be unaware of the basic structure of the Forces. Our country's ignorance of its defence forces is possibly by design rather than indifference. One of the theories is that after independence, the newly minted government took deliberate steps to undermine the importance of the army, downplaying its role in consolidating the various princely states, including Jammu and Kashmir (J and K). Perhaps there was a fear that the well-oiled and well-led machinery would replace the British.

But for a democracy of our size and given the times that we live in, it is important for every citizen to know more about national security, especially since it is the citizenry which eventually contributes to and is most affected by the state of the nation's security. I hope this series of articles would give readers an insight into security-related issues that affect all of us. In the first of this series, I want to discuss the challenges that our Forces are facing.

The Indian Armed Forces (I include the Border Security Force, Central Reserve Police Force, and other border security elements, though the million-strong Indian Army constitutes the largest component by far) are responsible for guarding a border across traditional and nuclear enemy nations (Pakistan and China); hostile and/or disturbed nations (Bangladesh, Myanmar, Nepal and Sri Lanka) and disputed areas like J and K. The latter alone uses up substantial troops to address the disturbance that has been raging for years. The same army is also required to tackle insurgency in the entire north-eastern region and train regularly for conventional battle scenarios in the western theatre against Pakistan and the eastern theatre against China and Bangladesh.

This army could also be called upon, and therefore trains, for overseas operations in Sri Lanka or Maldives (both have happened in the past), jungle warfare in some of the thickest jungles of the world, desert warfare in the second largest desert of the world, and ultra-high altitude warfare in Siachen glacier.

The Forces also have about 3,000 troops kept operationally ready for United Nations deployment. In addition, fighting units are expected to send officers to other paramilitary units and establishments such as the National Security Guard, Assam Rifles, Rashtriya Rifles, Research and Analysis Wing, Intelligence Bureau, Defence Research and Development Organisation, and for appointment as aide-de-camp (French for camp assistant) to the President and senior military officers.

The problem is there simply aren't enough leaders for the job.

A critical factor influencing the calibre of any army is leadership at the combat level. It is these combat leaders (lieutenants, captains, and majors) who lead troops into battle, grow into experienced veterans, and rise to occupy operational positions as colonels and then move to strategic levels as brigadiers and generals to shape strategy and doctrine. A typical fighting battalion consists of about 750 soldiers grouped into four companies of about 180 men and led by about 22 commissioned officers. These are leaders who join the army as lieutenants and work their way up the hierarchy. But the tap is drying at the entry level.

About 20 years ago, an army career was considered a close second to the civil services and hence attracted commensurate talent. Today, it's near the bottom of the totem pole. We can talk about the reasons till the cows come home, but that doesn't change the fact that both in quality and quantity, fighting units are facing up to 30 percent deficiency of junior leaders. Even the recently rediscovered NSG executed the Mumbai operations with these deficiencies.

It is obvious that the army cannot fight this dual challenge of increasing responsibilities and decreasing number of leaders—and something's got to give. The signs of stretch are showing on the organization, and it is only the incredible tradition of leadership in the Armed Forces that is holding the fort. But they need participative help from rest of the society. And perhaps the first step is to understand the issues of national defence and our role in that.

Corporate World Needs People from Armed Forces

A vast majority of officers and men leave with at least two decades of productive careers still ahead of them

In August, 2009, I read an insightful report by executive search firm Korn/Ferry on officers from the defence forces joining the corporate world. The study revealed that officers brought unique elements from the combat zone into business competition.

A vast majority of officers and men leave with at least two decades of productive careers still ahead of them. Most countries have learnt to exploit this incredible resource, and India is fast catching up. The Indian Army discharges approximately 1,500 officers every year. They range from short-service officers, with about seven years of experience, to those who have completed their pensionable service of around 20 years and are in their forties.

Some years ago, the army ran an advertising campaign on the exciting life of a combat soldier. It showed an officer barely into his 20s, commanding a tank squadron (1,500 horsepower company car), parachuting from an aeroplane (company jet), and leading a raid into enemy territory (foreign travel). That is just the tip of the iceberg. There are few professions, which hold leaders responsible for the lives of the men under their command, or where they have to lead men into death without ESOPs (employee stock ownership plan), pay hikes, or performance bonuses. Also, there is no other profession where men love (or hate) their leaders with such passionate fervour. Where one learns that there are no good units or bad units, just good or bad leaders. Where errors of judgement leave widows and orphans in their wake. This excellent grounding helps officers fit five basic role profiles.

The first is administration. During a typical career, an officer performs the role of managing resources and equipment worth several hundred crore rupees. He is responsible for the well-being and training of his men, planning logistics, controlling deployment, and coordinating exercises with other units and services. And he would be adept in process development with a keen sense of what could go wrong.

The second role flows from these experiences into HR and man management. During service, an officer is held accountable for the well-being of his men and their families. He is required to know what makes them tick, their individual strengths, weaknesses, and vulnerabilities. Good units groom their officers to know each soldier by his name, learn the language of the troops he commands, and motivate them in a manner that they best respond to. He literally has to get inside their heads and skins, and realize that every soldier is an individual, with individual problems and aspirations. Operations is another role where officers take like duck to water. They have spent years executing and making seemingly impossible plans happen. Their ability to multitask, high levels of energy, and 'can do' attitude makes them excellent operations and project managers. India's telecom revolution owes a lot to hundreds of signals officers, who helped roll out the grid that connects our country.

Security is a natural extension, ranging from physical and electronic security to high-end specialized roles such as counter-intelligence, fraud investigation, close protection of high value assets, disaster, and crisis management. Combat hones a sixth sense of perception and gives them an ability to be cool, calm and composed even in the face of extraordinary crisis.

The last role where many officers have proved their mettle is the holy grail of wealth creation. They have successfully found-ed and led companies in sectors ranging from consulting to retail. James McKinsey was an army officer and so was Sam Walton. Closer home, defence officers have headed business units, political ministries, and channels. They have been leading correspondents, authors, entrepreneurs, social activists, administrators, and thought leaders. The largest real estate developer and the harbinger of affordable airlines in India have both been defence forces officers.

With a decade in the army and the corporate world, I identify with much of this. But the hypothesis remains incomplete without highlighting where defence officers struggle in making the switch—from a cocooned life in the services to the competitiveness of the corporate environment.

First, is finance. In the services, officers learn to optimize the resources for output—but seldom visit the basic rules of finance and worry about rates of return on investment, a skill that is essential to handling profit and loss account responsibilities. Next, overbearing hierarchy is an operational requirement in the forces. In the corporate world, this can lead to a group of 'yes men'—convenient but not optimal. In his able lieutenants, every senior corporate leader looks for courage that will allow them to speak their mind. Much of the effort has to be put in by reporting seniors—who will let the career service officer realize that challenging a superior is not tantamount to indiscipline.

Marketing and business development also strike me as gaps. But these have less critical implications for most businesses. The defence ministry and several business schools are working to overcome these skill gaps through programmes for officers.

All said and done, it is hard to replace men who have mettle and a winning attitude. I am reminded of an army officer, who was asked one of those favourite interview questions by a business tycoon, 'So, what has been the greatest challenge of your life?' The officer reflected for a few moments and said matter-of-factly, 'Well, people had been trying to kill me and my men, you know. I guess just surviving with my men, alive, was a challenge alright.' Here's to old soldiers, who never die!

Some Ways in Which We Can
Thank the Armed Forces

Soldiers draw their strength and morale from the society they help protect

It has been almost a year since Mumbai was attacked by 10 terrorists who tore through our lives and ravaged us. For most citizens of Mumbai, that attack was possibly the closest they ever came to confronting the dangers and the violence that men in uniform have to tackle every day. These are sons who come from remote villages, brothers who choose hard careers, and fathers who don't see their children 10 months in a year—in a good year.

My thoughts go back to 27 November, the second day of the attack, when National Security Guard commandos stormed into the Taj and Oberoi hotels. Like every Indian watching that scene, my heart swelled with pride. When India sent its best to take out the worst that our enemies could throw at us.

When I learnt what those commandos had to face and how they opened at least 500 rooms, fighting non-stop for 72 hours with no food or water, and neutralized every single one of the terrorists, without a single collateral damage—a feat that is unparalleled in counter-terrorist operations—I was proud to belong to the same country whose badge those soldiers wore on their uniforms. The deafening cheer of the crowds that saw them returning after the mission told me that I was not alone in that raw emotion of pride.

This is not just about the NSG though. It is about our forces battling in Jammu and Kashmir, in the North-east, in the searing deserts, and freezing mountains. It is about troops who rush to the rescue during natural calamities, who make it possible to hold elections in midst of floods and Naxal violence. It is about young majors who leave behind widows and toddlers. It is about police constables who hold a blazing AK-47 barrel in their bare hands so that we can sleep well.

Most people would not do that job for a million dollars. They do it for a lot less. So one year later, what have we done to reinforce support, admiration, and gratitude to our troops in uniform? How have we shown that we are proud of them and wish that they will always be victorious? Sure, we could contribute to the funds raised for those who died and we have. We could watch a few programmes about cricketers visiting those troops and we have.

But a year later, we must realize that national security is no longer an issue we can be non-participative about. We need to put our skin into the game and prove beyond doubt that we stand behind our troops every inch of the way, just like they have stood between us and our enemies.

Many years ago, a general narrated this telling story about the Indian Peace-Keeping Force's (IPKF) induction into Sri Lanka. The initial days of the mobilization were hurried and massive number of troops were being pushed in with minimal logistics. Soldiers were tasked to be prepared for combat on landing and carried several days of cooked meals on person. They were burdened with heavy equipment as they trudged towards the transport aircraft.

During one such occasion at Thiruvananthapuram airport, a plane's back blast caught a soldier off guard and his ruck-sack blew open, strewing its contents all over the tarmac. The soldier ran one way and the other trying to collect his belongings, food packets, and letters from home. Since Thiru-vananthapuram was a civilian airport, there was a crowd of onlookers who were amused by this soldier's frantic dashes and couldn't control their laughter.

And it was at that precise point that the general realized that IPKF was doomed to fail. Any country that sends its soldiers into combat without its solid reaffirmation behind them is bound to fail.

A couple of years ago, I was on a flight in the US, when the air hostess announced that two US army personnel were returning from their tour of duty in Iraq.

The entire aircraft, without exception, gave them a standing ovation which didn't stop for several minutes and until most passengers had personally thanked the two overwhelmed soldiers.

That is a fundamental requisite of combat. Soldiers don't draw their strength and morale from equipment or resources. They draw it from the society and the community they help protect. And the kind of support which the society commits when one of their warriors falls in the line of duty. This is why soldiers place their lives on the line. And if we have to avoid the epitaph of a soft state, this is the psyche we need to cultivate as a nation. However, we cannot think our way into doing new things; instead, we need to do our way into a new way of thinking. So what can we do to support our troops? Surprisingly, quite a lot with little effort.

One of the areas that the Armed Forces struggle with is resettlement of ex-servicemen into the mainstream. Officers and men who are barely into their late 30s need help. It is not about sops or reservations; instead, they need skills to translate military competencies into corporate ones.

Indian Institutes of Management and several premier business schools run short MBA programmes for officers who are leaving the forces. As corporates and individuals, we owe it to them to volunteer as faculty. Corporates could conduct similar programmes for ex-servicemen within their premises. They could simply decide to hire a fixed percentage from retiring soldiers.

Non-governmental organizations could fix a certain percentage of their vacancies for children orphaned during operations, individuals could adopt the responsibility of assisting a widow or siblings in skilling and finding a job. Companies could encourage their CSR programme to be oriented towards the forces. They could also encourage their employees to consider stints as short service officers or join the territorial army or the civil defence. In other countries, companies and private citizens adopt battalions or individual soldiers and help them through their careers and thereafter. Frankly, it is not about the monetary assistance, though that helps. It is about saying thank you for laying down your today for our tomorrow.

Understanding National Security and Our Role in Safeguarding Our Own Environments

How Defence Spending Can Benefit the Economy

Most technologies that were designed for warfare have
extensive non-military use. The Internet,
nuclear power, space programmes, deep oceanic
mapping, and transcontinental communications
are just some of the examples

It is a universal belief that defence expenditure is a waste of
valuable resources. In an absolute sense, that may be a fact.
In an ideal world, even a fraction of the resources being
spent on defence globally could solve many of the world's
problems. Having said that, mankind has always been and will
probably always be, in conflict. Countries will be at war and
communities will constantly battle each other. If anything, this
attrition will only exacerbate as conflict follows the universal
principle of scarcity—that as resources reduce and contenders
increase, there will be war.

But the moneys that a country allocates to building war capabilities also benefit it in many ways. In this article, I want to
talk about how resources allocated for primarily 'destructive'
purposes can and do spur economic growth and well-being.

Almost all major inventions, discoveries, and management
philosophies owe a lot to warfare. If the technology wasn't
invented specifically for war, it was most certainly scaled and
mass-produced for it. Radar, sonar, communication equipment, computers, wireless, missiles, rockets, assembly line
production efficiencies, logistics, air transportation, and
countless other technologies and processes have their origins
in defence labs and battlefields. Most technologies that were
designed for warfare have extensive non-military use. The
Internet, nuclear power, space programmes, deep oceanic

mapping, and transcontinental communications are just some of the examples.

The second benefit that the armed forces give to the community is the pool of disciplined, well-trained young men and women. The Indian Army discharges some 50,000 trained soldiers back to the hinterland. These men bring with them a national outlook, skills that the army taught them, and the secular world view they have experienced during their stint in the forces.

Thousands of ex-servicemen have returned to their native villages and started entrepreneurial ventures leveraging their competencies.

The defence procurement and the offset policy is another example of how our defence expenditure can contribute to nation-building. The current defence budget has a procurement component of Rs 54,800 crore, which will be used to purchase state-of-the-art equipment. Around 70 percent of this is in the form of imports. The procurement policy lays down the provision of 'offsets', which essentially mandates that the seller of the armament has to buy or provision up to 50 percent of the cost of the weapon platform from Indian manufacturers. This ensures that a sizeable percentage of money spent on defence procurement is ploughed back into the economy. The offset structure also incentivizes collaboration with Indian partners to indigenize substantial parts of the equipment to fulfil the offset obligation, thereby facilitating technology transfer into Indian industries. Global firms are expected to channelize up to $20 billion in 10 years into India. This creates very interesting opportunities.

While the purpose of the policy and, therefore, the aim of the weapon's suppliers would be to try and indigenize the equipment, three distinct benefits will accrue from this arrangement.

Firstly, in a pursuit to increase the indigenous component of equipment, sellers will need to transfer technology. This will serve to jump-start private sector firms into the defence space, which until now was largely the domain of government establishments. Secondly, as the process of offsetting starts in earnest, it will lead the seller and his Indian partner down the road into 'offshoring'. This means the weapon platform could be built at a lower cost enabling it to become globally competitive and establish India as a global defence production and service hub. Thirdly, the entry of global firms and defence funds into India will create and rejuvenate an entire ecosystem of tier II and tier III manufacturing firms. Given that defence spending is largely recession-proof, this infusion of funds and assured order books will do for the manufacturing sector what the business process outsourcing/knowledge process outsourcing industry did for the IT offshoring industry.

The government has begun to encourage private participation in defence. Listing of select group of firms as raksharatnas and the government's willingness to fund major development work with private firms will further contribute to growth of indigenous defence and ancillary manufacturing capability.

Our defence budget also consists of regular revenue expenditure in the form of salaries, allowances, and sustenance costs of maintaining an army. Food has to be bought, roads have to be built, vehicles need to ply, and the agricultural produce of several thousand villages goes to maintaining garrisons stationed all over the country. An entire ecosystem thrives on maintaining and mobilizing the defence forces. Cantonment towns are examples of cities which have been fuelled by defence establishments that literally created them.

Economic historians attribute the meteoric rise of the US industries to the thousands of discharged military men from World War II, who brought leadership qualities, process orientation and a 'can do' attitude back from the war zone. Indian defence forces can play a similar role in constructive nation-building in addition to its primary task of providing national security, which is an essential component of economic growth.

Know the Dangers of Ignoring Those Street Children

Most societies tend to look at issues only when they spiral out of control

In September, 2009, papers in the UK reported a horrifying incident that took place in the mining village of Edlington. Two children, aged nine and 11, were tortured to within an inch of their lives.

These children were lured into a waste ground, robbed, beaten, burnt with cigarettes, sexually humiliated, strangled with barbed wire, and stabbed while being told that they were going to die. One of the boys was found covered in blood and the other had been hit in the head and left for dead.

Repulsive as any crime on children inherently is, this doesn't sound unusual so far. The extraordinary aspect about this incident, however, is that the perpetrators of this heinous crime were aged 10 and 11!

These feral children were raised by a violent and drunken father, who beat them and made them fight each other, and a drug-addicted mother. She had seven children from three fathers and abandoned them to the point where the kids foraged and fed themselves from garbage bins.

The Daily Mail called it the symptom of a social and cultural emergency. Suddenly the guilt shifts from the individuals—in this instance, young boys—to society at large.

I use the incident to highlight the responsibility that society has towards creating a secure environment for its future generations. And this is a challenge that India faces with respect to its internal security.

How do we make our citizens realize the role they have to play at an individual level in promoting inclusive growth? This is not about moral social service. It is about ensuring the survivability of our children.

Next time you are on the streets, look around. You'll see hundreds of street kids who forage, fight and claw their way through life, inch by inch, day after day. You will see babies, drugged and farmed out for begging, children mutilated, injured in accidents, and beaten regularly by motorists. As I said, this article is not about moral responsibility. It is about asking a very practical question: What do you think happens to these graduates of the vicious school of street life? Those who survive are deeply scarred, sadistic, with no regard for social values or at least values as we—those who have had a privileged existence—define them.

They become fodder for criminal gangs, drug peddlers, violent crime, and terrorism. And the society sets the police on them when they have crossed the point of no return. But we stand by and watch, while they are systematically tottering towards that Rubicon.

Human trafficking is the third largest criminal business in the world. It is also intricately linked to the first two, drugs and illegal arms trade. And this happens right under our noses.

It is ironic that while we are appalled and judgemental about historically barbaric practices such as slave trading or apartheid, human trafficking is a thriving 21st century industry that cannot possibly flourish without being condoned by society or connivance by government.

Most societies tend to look at problems and issues only when they spiral out of control. And then they seek to attack the manifestation of the problem rather than the root cause. It is my firm belief that the widening gap between the two segments of society—the have-nots and the give-nots —is a powder keg waiting for a spark.

And while that has many expressions, there is nothing as shameful as a whole generation of children abandoned to fend for themselves or exploited for commercial benefit. Most citizens can do very little to prevent drug or arms trade. But the exploitation of children is a different matter. It is a clear and present danger to our own children.

Make no mistake—that badly scarred kid begging on the other side of the car window is going to grow into a menace soon. At best—for you, that is—she will be forced into lifelong prostitution or begging and at worst he will turn into a hardened criminal. You might be able to shoo him away now or roll up the window and pretend you don't see him. But that won't make him go away. Your child will have to face them when they grow up.

And when they do, for three reasons, my bet is on the kid outside the window. First, the kid outside has been hurt, starved, violated, and persecuted. He doesn't understand the concept of pity, mercy, love, or tolerance. He has the same regard for society as society has for him—nothing!

Second, the kid outside the window outnumbers your children by several thousands to one. No matter how tough your child is, she can't beat those odds. And last, but most importantly, the kid outside has nothing to lose. What can you do to him that life hasn't already dished out, while you stood by?

This is the single biggest challenge when dealing with terrorists or criminals. Try and recollect the last time you burnt or hurt yourself. Now multiply that a million times and you have an idea of what it takes to strap a pack of explosives around yourself and blow it up. Sure, there are instances of well-to-do children growing into bad cases but those are exceptions proving the rule, that every society will get back what it sows.

Terrorism may begin with an ideology, but it turns into a business, and finally into a racket. And the way to fix it is by breaking the racket and then addressing the ideology. I am a believer of direct action. And I am convinced that if any scourge affects a society, it is because the society allows it.

Exploitation of children is a harbinger to criminalization of future generations. And it happens around us because we allow it. Every traffic signal in every major city is infested with a franchised begging model, right under the noses of every official and citizen. And not only do we allow it, we also feed that monster.

I pity the naivete of anyone who does not see the racket for what it is or the debilitating effect it will have on our future generations. I equally question the conscience of a society that ignores it, of the media which does not hammer away at it until it stops, or the citizenry which is not outraged by it.

Because all it takes for evil to flourish is that good men stand by and do nothing.

— ◈ —

After 26/11, Changes in India's Security Mindset

While security is almost a birthright and a prerequisite to all other elements of development, aiming to improve it in isolation is naive

Each one of us probably remembers exactly where we were during those three days of the horrific attacks on Mumbai. Some, like me, lost close friends in the attacks and we all felt collective helplessness waiting outside the Taj and Trident hotels for the commando operations to end. A year later, the most pressing question doing the rounds is—are we better prepared?

In the days that followed, authorities from all over the world poured into India to advise us on dealing with terrorists. People became experts on the matter of security and even Page 3 regulars had an opinion on the subject. At one point, so many security experts from a certain country had gathered in India that I was getting a little concerned about the safety of that country! Several reports were written, promises made, and plans designed. But by and large, the general lament seems to be that nothing has changed.

I see the situation differently. The beginning of any change is a point in time, determined more by the events that follow it rather than the point itself. To that extent, the US had 9/11, the UK had 11/7, and perhaps India had 26/11. And while it would be fashionable to argue that very little has improved, I think we must appreciate a few aspects about security before we judge the extent of progress that has been made.

Before we proceed, I want to clarify that I believe India is wanting in its desired standard of security. That is a given. The question we are asking today is not whether India is secure—but whether the needle has moved in the last 12 months.

While security is almost a birthright and a prerequisite to all other elements of development, aiming to improve it in isolation is naïve. After an incident like 26/11, the people will understandably clamour for activities which assure better preparedness next time around. So visible actions such as creating NSG (National Security Guard) hubs, modernizing the police force, and improving intelligence are all important and legitimate expectations. But to expect that security standards can improve dramatically in a matter of 12 months is a tall order simply because of the scale and complexity of the requirements. It is a bit like saying we need to be prepared for the next earthquake in 12 months after the last one has hit us.

So what has changed? I believe India witnessed a watershed with respect to its security mindset with 26/11—and the way we view internal security has altered fundamentally. And this is not limited to a small set of people, i.e., those who were close to the events of 26/11, or involved with India's security infrastructure, or simply political or social observers. There is a noticeable shift in every possible stakeholder's mindset—and this augurs well for the shape of things to come.

Let's begin with our citizens who have indicated that they have had enough. And this is not about candlelight vigils. Instead, it is about a realization that better security comes at some personal sacrifice. In the one year that has passed after 26/11, cooperation and empathy with security staff at airports, hotels and other public places is a telling indicator that the common man is happy to pull his weight when it comes to suffering inconveniences for better security. No longer do Indians make faces or throw tantrums or even object to delays caused by security measures.

Secondly, companies have got into the act. In the year after 26/11, more firms than ever before have made substantial investments in terms of security apparatus, personnel, and training. Bodies such as the Confederation of Indian Industry and Federation of Indian Chambers of Commerce and Industry have added security to their agenda and conducted programmes for their members and the general public.

Thirdly, the media has been supportive of the enhanced attention to security issues. In fact, it has played a proactive role in creating momentum and making security everyone's business. By highlighting how easy it was for 26/11 to happen, they have raised the bar for the future.

And lastly, the government response has been heartening as well. There wasn't any serious attempt to cover up failures after 26/11. Rapid leadership changes were effected. Leaders with track records were put on the job, resources were mobilized, equipment was procured, and new establishments were raised. For the first time, we saw no hesitation on account of foreign relations or political correctness for the government to mince its words. The message is unequivocal—whether against Pakistan for supporting terrorists or dealing with the home-grown Maoists. The time for pussy-footing is over.

Meaningful preparedness of any sort takes time to mature. And many of these steps, especially those involving the more elaborate measures such as intelligence and modernization programmes, will have to go through their gestation periods to start yielding results. But the heartening factor is the first traces of a shifting mindset—the underlying determination that we are ready to do whatever it takes to make it happen—a sentiment that wasn't as assertive during the terrorist provocations that occurred in the past, including the audacious attack on Parliament. And that, perhaps, is the best indicator that a lot has changed in a year after 26/11.

— ◆ —

Raising Social Consciousness
is the First Step

While terrorism may have become a label for fundamentalist activists, stamping it out begins with zero tolerance towards all unacceptable behaviour

February, 2010 saw the end of a 14-month hiatus from terror attacks. Fifteen lives were lost in a bomb blast in Pune, underscoring the sad fact that each day we move from the last strike is a day closer to the next one.

I want to talk about an aspect which is particularly relevant for a society to be co-opted into the battle against terrorism. About realizing that fighting terrorism begins much closer than we think.

Twenty-three years ago, Second Lieutenant Alok Singh was commissioned into the Indian Army. Those were turbulent years for our forces. Terrorism was still raging in Punjab and we had a full-blown war in Sri Lanka. Singh was launched straight into operations in some of the toughest combat spots as part of the Indian Peace Keeping Force in Sri Lanka. And he showed the finest tradition of the Indian Army winning the Veer Chakra, one of the country's highest gallantry awards.

In February, 2010, Singh was killed in a hit-and-run accident in upmarket south Delhi. That fact in itself is unremarkable, given that thousands of people die in accidents in India each year.

What was incredible was that this war hero lay on the road bleeding for over three hours before he was taken to a hospital. He left behind ageing parents, a wife and two young boys whose world was shattered within minutes.

Like all other families that lose their loved ones, there was bewilderment as to why the hundreds of passers-by, motorists and pedestrians, who saw Singh mangled on the road, didn't help him.

I can appreciate the fear in the driver, who actually hit him and ran, but I find it hard to understand the apathy of those who followed and did nothing.

On 13 February, 2010, a bomb explosion took place in Pune. A week later, Maoist rebels slaughtered 25 paramilitary personnel and three days later, killed 12 more, but on the very same day, prominent English-language dailies led with the news that India was indeed No. 1 in cricket.

Lest we choose the easy way out, and chide the newspapers, let us be clear that they are a mirror of the society, not its conscience keepers.

I like cricket as much as the next guy, but when a nation reeling under devastating attacks accords priority to a national pastime over national security, I think it is time to join the dots and extrapolate the big picture.

Just what does it take for us to be shaken out of this sense of individual and collective apathy? At what point will there be a realization that security and safety cannot be left to a few million soldiers and paramilitary personnel. And that zero tolerance must begin with behavioural changes at the very basic levels and not grandiose strategies across borders.

In his book *The Tipping Point*, Malcom Gladwell chronicled the saga of New York city being brought back from the brink of crime-ridden collapse.

The starting point of Mayor Rudolph Giuliani's battle against the literal underworld of New York tube service was a refusal to accept dirty trains. He understood the concept of the 'broken window', which postulates that when the window of an abandoned house is first broken, and no one fixes it, then more windows get broken.

The broken windows act as a signal that no one is in charge and so pretty soon the entire building is defaced. Next the vagrants and dope dealers start hanging around this building and before you know it, it becomes the crime street headquarters. But it all starts with that first broken window, which wasn't fixed as soon as it was broken.

The condoning of that basic act was the starting point of social degeneration. It is high time that we identify our broken windows. They could be something as simple as being uncompromising on traffic regulations and keeping at it until there is a cultural shift. Until red light jumping, speeding, lane breaking, and every act of impudence and disregard for social norms is stamped out.

As a matter of fact—it should ideally be something simple, almost banal, but requiring resolute steadfastness to eradicate. Zero tolerance needs to begin at ground zero.

While terrorism may have become a label for fundamentalist activists, stamping it out begins with zero tolerance towards all unacceptable behaviour. Because if we don't pay attention to how these dots are joining, we may soon have no choice, but to tolerate.

— ◆ —

Can't Afford to Ignore the Enemy at the Gates

As parents and citizens, we are making the mistake of focusing on our 'sphere of interest' rather than our 'sphere of influence'

Given my line of work, I'm often asked questions such as 'Is it safe to travel by planes these days?' Or more recent ones such as 'Which city do you think the terrorists will target next?'

Such questions illustrate the subtle peculiarity of human behaviour—that we focus on risks that are distant and out of our immediate influence rather than those that constantly threaten us and our loved ones. There is no doubt that the unpredictability of terrorist attacks and the media fixation on them have contributed to terror getting such high mindshare. Nevertheless, you or your loved ones are exposed to far greater risk from more mundane everyday deliberate attacks such as rape, mugging, robbery, assault, and molestation—often times by those whom you personally know—than being involved in a terrorist strike.

One could argue that such social crimes are a feature of banana republics or poorer countries which cannot afford to spend on security of their society. So let us consider the example of a country which lost more lives to gunshot wounds in 2008-09 than the total casualties during the Vietnam War (around 65,000). Where 75 women are raped every hour and around 70 children are killed by parents—every week! And around four million children abused in 2009 (that is around 11,000 every day). A country where more women go to the casualty ward of hospitals because of injuries caused by their husbands or partners—than car accidents, robberies, and rape combined.

I could go on, but you get the point. The country being discussed is the US—unarguably a nation that spends more on defence and security than any other in the world.

I make this observation to point out a simple fact. Violence and threats are closer than we think and you are far more likely to be exposed to a life-threatening situation from everyday circumstances than high-voltage events such as plane bombings or terrorist shootouts. As Gavin Becker, an expert on violent behaviour, points out, modern society spends far more resources and time improving its capabilities for rare conflicts than avoiding everyday dangerous situations.

So we check several million individuals each year for weapons on a flight, in cinemas and hotels, but we neglect the credentials of servants who work in our homes, security guards who are on our premises, or staff who are supposed to care for aged parents. We trust complete strangers with our homes and our children with relatives and friends, despite the fact that almost all child molestation is done by relatives or known people. And as the recent scandals rocking the Catholic world show, sometimes by the very people supposed to be protecting them.

As parents and citizens, we are making the mistake of focusing on 'our sphere of interest' rather than our 'sphere of influence'.

This attitude towards security has two disadvantages, one obvious and the other subtle, but equally devastating. The obvious one is that the resources, be it in the form of deployment of assets, education or awareness, start focusing on the wrong things. Learning about the Mumbai attacks is unlikely to be of much use to your daughter, but knowledge about date rape modus operandi could possibly save her life. And yet, the average teenager is bombarded with information about the former, but has no clue about the latter. Similarly armchair 'experts' comment authoritatively about the flaws of security frameworks in public places such as hotels and airports, but don't bother heeding signs that their children are hooked on narcotics or are being sexually abused. In both such instances, parents are invariably the last to know and are often shocked by how long it took them to discover it.

The subtler disadvantage of this obsessive global focus on security is that the pattern of threats to your immediate family is entirely different from that of, say, a bomb explosion or a plane hijack. For instance, no terrorist announces a bomb attack or his intention to assassinate an important person, but almost all cases of domestic violence, peer abuse, sexual assaults, and premeditated murder are preceded by verbal and even written threats or warnings. As are suicides—to which we lose more people every day—than all the deaths of the Mumbai attack. And this is what I find ironic that parents who ask me concerned questions about the safety of a city, very rarely instil a sense of the need to wear helmets (or use contraceptives) in their children.

Personally, I believe a sense of security starts at home and in the immediate circles of influence. Our children are entering a world where school, college and workplace violence, stalkers, aggressive bullies, traffic accidents, peer-pressured dangerous behaviour, and sexual risks are far more likely to be encountered than a terrorist attack. And while there is no doubt that we ought to be actively interested in the security environment in our sphere of interest, it must not be at the cost of ignoring the enemy at the gates.

— ◈ —

The Persistence of an Old Problem

Recent terror attacks show their perpetrators can
strike at will and only a systemic response can halt them

Recently, a delegation of Fortune 10 conglomerates was on its
way to India when executives received an alert from a global
risk advisory firm, advising them to cancel their trip. Although
the visit had been planned months in advance and several
relationships were at stake, they turned back. Their offices
communicated a message that we ought to start heeding.

In view of the unsafe situation in India, the world's
investment influencers are reluctant to come here until things
improve.

Business communities recognize that terrorism cannot be
eliminated in an absolute sense. They also appreciate that
India has unique challenges in terms of size, scale, a consensual
(and often contradictory) democratic process resulting in
organizational sluggishness. However, six highly visible attacks
since 26/11 without any significant breakthrough in any of
them, wears down even the most ardent advocates of the India
opportunity story. And unlike Indian citizens, the global
community has other alternatives which they have begun
exploring.

So this is not just about the dozen dead and scores injured—
though that in itself is abominable. It is about realizing that
terrorism and internal security issues are critically threatening
the one redeeming factor that India has going in its favour—its
growth potential. And terrorists know that while explosions
in the hinterland don't scare the global business community—
the ones in high courts and marketplaces do and hence they
will continue pounding such high -visibility targets to damage
the economy.

It is time for the country's economic community to recognize that terrorism and internal security issues are going to throw wrenches into their plans with increasing regularity.

Terrorism is, of course, one of the manifestations of several causes (religious fundamentalism being just one) and both the expression and the cause need to be addressed systematically. However, the wake-up call should be the impact that internal security issues have on the economy, psyche and the morale of the country and its potential investors.

Though details and the intent of the perpetrators of the Delhi high court attack are still unclear, this attack in particular should be more alarming for two reasons. Firstly, coming less than four months from the previous explosion in the same premises, it demonstrates the audacity of the perpetrators who were not deterred by the higher levels of security in the aftermath of the previous attempt.

More importantly, this strike was not for any overarching strategic purpose but a very tactical demand—i.e. preventing the law from carrying out its course, reminiscent of the Kandahar hijack.

A plausible extrapolation could be that terrorists will begin such attacks for specific tactical demands in this new format of compellence. The infuriation after such attacks is now all too familiar.

However, exasperation leads to knee-jerk responses that do not really improve the situation. The reality is that we are trying to defeat a nimble enemy with archaic systems, processes and mindsets that have their roots in the era of conventional warfare. In doing so, we forget that the raison d'etre of asymmetric warfare is to thwart a superior enemy by bypassing the latter's strengths.

There is a fable of a swarm of bees which attacked an elephant and eventually killed it. Their stings in themselves were only an irritant to the mammoth, but the beast literally beat itself to death hitting its own body trying to kill the bees. We are in a similar situation now. The answer perhaps lies in recasting our strategy to counter the nimbleness of the terrorists with some structural changes of our own.

Anyone with even a remote familiarity of government processes knows the near impossibility of rapidness, especially during creation of new capability.

Each terrorist incident is followed by strident demands for speedy ramp up, but barely weeks later every attempt at capability creation is entangled in well-intended but antiquated processes, attempts to garner absolute consensus and even insinuations of foul play.

A place to look for answers could be countries that faced and addressed similar threats, factoring the indigenization that India requires. The US, which is often quoted as a benchmark for preventing subsequent attacks, was in a similar situation before 9/11.

Different departments and activist groups were pulling in multiple directions with a focus on their own agendas. However, they were able to build consensus across disparate stakeholders within and outside the country.

That requires singularity of national purpose and a rallying point. Given the contrarian pulls of various stakeholders, perhaps that rallying point should be the economic damage that India will continue to suffer, unless we address terrorism in a systematic manner. This will require rising above parochial agendas and establishing economy as the common denominator whose debilitation goes far beyond the shock waves of bombs.

We must also realize that for a country which faces a multitude of threats, looking for the perfect solution will prevent implementation of a good one.

In the wake of the current wave of civil activism the establishment is wary of taking any step that has the potential to be torn down on some imperfection or the other. But again taking lessons from countries which have achieved results, we must make a beginning and focus on the deficiencies we are replacing rather than criticize the ideal we are not achieving.

Pirates of the Gulf of Aden

An explosive mix of ecological destruction and plunder
has led to piracy in Somalia. It will be hard to end it

Over the last decade, Somalia has become synonymous with
piracy. Several countries, including India, have been affected
directly or indirectly because of this menace. Despite patrolling and intervention by security forces of many countries,
Somali pirates have exacted several hundred million dollars in
ransom, held over a thousand people as hostages and disrupted trade worth $12 billion annually. The cost of keeping naval
channels safe, security on ships, delays in sailing time, and
increased insurance premiums all add up to a sum that has to
be borne by consumers. Security measures, however, address
only one issue—and perhaps at the wrong end of the stick. To
appreciate why the combined might of several countries fails
to check this threat, it is important to understand the root of
the problem rather than its manifestation.

Somalia—like several other African countries—has been
ravaged by war, famine, and acute deprivation for decades.
When United Nations (UN) forces withdrew from Somalia,
the country turned into a 'failed' state virtually overnight.
With the collapse of any credible government, the Somali navy
ceased to be an effective force and the country's territorial
waters became happy hunting ground for industrial fishing
vessels from all over the world.

Unscrupulous and indiscriminate fishing—which included
devastating methods such as deep-sea dredging—destroyed all
marine life decimating the oceanic ecosystem. Somali fishermen, who had for centuries practised eco-friendly and traditional fishing methods, were no match for the powerful fishing mafias.

When word about this unprotected haven got around, Somali waters were further ravaged by dumping of radioactive and toxic material all along its coastline, damaging marine life. As if this weren't enough, the 2004 tsunami washed up contaminated waste right to Somali shores, sounding the death knell for millions of Somalis who depended on the sea for subsistence.

The first instance of 'piracy' began when the deprived Somali fishermen started confronting the industrial fishing ships and were obviously beaten back. However, this led to the fishermen teaming up with battle-hardened gunmen who were in plentiful supply, thanks to the decades of civil war. A lethal combine was formed between fishermen who knew the waters like the back of their hand and fighters for whom the ubiquitous AK-47 was an extension of their body.

Warlords, especially in southern Somalia, seized this income opportunity and turned piracy into military campaigns. The raiding parties now had automatic weapons, rocket launchers, high-powered outboard motors, and state-of-the-art navigation and communication devices. Pay-offs of up to $5 million have been obtained for the release of individual ships, and delivery of ransom has included sophisticated methods such as airdropping of cash over high seas.

For the starved Somalian economy, the pickings were simply too rich to resist. The Gulf of Aden is the jugular for most shipping in the southern hemisphere and is especially vital for India. What started out as an outraged protest has turned into a billion dollar industry with low investment.

In 2008, the world started getting its act together, with the UN empowering naval interceptors to enter Somali waters in hot pursuit. Large flotillas are now escorted by destroyers, but there are simply too many ships and not enough sheriffs to ride shotgun.

In response, the pirates leverage time-tested tools of guerilla warfare. Agility is laced with ruthlessness to send a message that it is cheaper to settle the ransom than to involve authorities. A typical raid begins by identifying and stalking a potential vessel from a safe distance using radars. At an opportune time, usually during the night, fast attack craft approach the vessel from multiple directions and overpower the defenceless crew, sometimes killing and maiming them. Next, the vessel is rigged with explosives to prevent storming by security forces. This is a strong deterrence because it uses the crew as human shields and also threatens an environmental disaster.

This deadlock has the same elements as many security issues facing the world. An impoverished community is pushed over the edge by the rapacious greed of a few. Fragile environments and meagre livelihoods are destroyed with disregard to people who rightfully own and depend on them. When those communities rise in retaliation, the world is outraged and brings its heavy-handed (and horribly expensive) might to tackle the surface problem, while continuing to ignore its root cause. This same script is played out time and again, be it forced relocation of coastal fishermen in Sri Lanka after the tsunami, purportedly for their safety—where five-star hotels were built—denying them access to the sea, or spraying of chemicals in Afghanistan to destroy the poppy crop without providing an alternative source of income.

Even as you read this, pirates are holding nine vessels with more than 240 hostages. Their beat has increased way beyond the Somali waterline into the high seas, often as far as the Kenyan coast. Piracy continues to exacerbate, costing the world billions of dollars. And yet it all started when poor fishermen were denied their livelihood. It is time for us to realize that the world is one village and no matter how distant the problem seems to be when it begins—unless addressed immediately with foresight—it lands at our doorstep quickly.

The Resource Wars of the Future

As resources dwindle and demands increase, conflicts will be exacerbated; there simply isn't enough for all

War originated as a planned and coordinated form of theft about 10,000 years ago. From the time early man began farming and hunting, tribes that could not grow food or had surplus to barter began raiding other communities that produced food. This was more difficult than hunting animals as their adversaries were equally intelligent and learnt to defend themselves.

The raiding tribe's strategy depended on attacking defenceless or, at least weaker, tribes at specific times of the year. At the same time, defending tribes began organizing themselves to repel raiders with better emplacements, obstacles, and deception. Eventually some tribes focused on farming and others on raiding. While the former created and developed ecosystems for better agricultural yields, storage methods and bartering, the latter developed efficiency in war, communication, and fast transportation.

Wars are initiated for many reasons. It may be to consolidate federated tribes as Genghis Khan did or due to ideological divides such as in the US Civil War or for 'living space' as in the case of Nazi Germany's concept of Lebensraum. War can also break out because of underlying geopolitical schisms as in many African or East European countries. Another possible reason can be ethnic divides such as in the case of Rwanda or the oppression of minorities in Sri Lanka. Whatever may be the claimed reason, the real and base purpose for all war is the desire to control resources in situations when there are more claimants than the available resource.

This brings us to a worrying conundrum. Mankind has been proliferating with scant regard to the planet's capacity to sustain the consumerist lifestyle that we take for granted.

More perturbing, however, are the patterns of consumption. The United Nations Development Programme's 2011 Human Development Report reads like a prologue to apocalypse. Human consumption—which has a direct bearing on the planet's capability to sustain and replenish itself—is at an all-time high and shows no signs of abating. Our requirements of energy, water, food and living space are fast outpacing the planet's capability to provide them. Nearly 1.3 billion people are directly affected by agricultural depletion, forestry, fishing, hunting, and foraging. Millions more will be affected because of rising water levels caused by global warming.

Contamination of water has displaced more humans than all wars put together and new incurable strains of diseases are incubating in a hot and crowded world. A few hundred years ago, when space or resources became a constraint, tribes just moved to new locations. But now, the earth is full. There simply aren't enough resources for all, especially as a small percentage of our species is consuming more than 80 percent of the world's resources, creating an existential threat for others.

This essentially boils down to a simple formula. As resources dwindle and demands increase, conflicts will exacerbate. We will see more wars, violence, and devastation in the coming decades. Wars for basic supplies such as water and food are already on in some regions of the world. And several other ideological or political conflicts are simply resource wars masquerading under different euphemisms.

The situation is especially worrying for India. As a nation, we are surrounded by failing states and hostile countries. We need to maintain the second largest army in the world and face the largest one as our foe. We have fought major wars across three fronts and have been facing a proxy war for two decades. We spend nearly 2 percent of our national output on defence while struggling to provide for education and healthcare. In addition to external threats, we are in the epicentre of global terror and have several internal security issues —the biggest being ultra-Left violence that according to some reports also has elements of a resource war.

Nation-building activities directly and indirectly affect millions of people. Healthcare, education, infrastructure, employment, energy distribution, agriculture and other sectors have economic implications, especially when there are several stakeholders, all of whom can't benefit equitably. Even if care were taken to be fair to all, several would have to undergo a forced change in their way of living, which is always a cause for dissent. Unfortunately, in these times when the world is embroiled in multiple crises, the only way to draw attention to the issue of dissent is violence. This is especially true for the weaker and minority groups for whom asymmetric war is increasingly becoming the favoured option.

Our next generation of business, political, and bureaucratic leaders and managers will be confronted with security related situations more frequently. But our education, awareness, and planning systems do not factor their security implication. This deficiency constantly forces us to expend far more resources in trying to confront and contain the dissent rather than preventing it in the first place. In some situations, the latter option is simply not possible because of severe depletion of resources.

Careful husbanding of our resources is essential to balance development and security. Ignorance of this symbiotic relationship is probably the biggest security risk that our nation faces.

— ◈ —

Terror against Women

The solution lies in providing a strong support structure
to victims and high deterrence to potential perpetrators

This month, another victim of 'terrorism' succumbed to her
injuries, which included broken arms, smashed head and
human bite marks. She was all of two years old. During the
same time, two women were abducted in broad daylight,
gang-raped and thrown away, one of them just a schoolgirl.
Even if the National Crime Records Bureau figures were to be
taken as comprehensive, which, given the low rates of reporting they certainly aren't, a woman is raped in India every 24
minutes and this crime is rising faster than murder, robbery,
and kidnapping.

Ironically, the supposedly safer urban areas lead in rape
cases and the national capital holds the ignominious distinction of accounting for nearly half of all rape cases in urban
India. Our country that touts youth as its economic power-
house also holds the world record for child abuse and trafficking. And just to complete the gory story, nearly 40 percent of
married women suffer some form of physical or sexual abuse
at the hands of their husbands and in-laws. Undoubtedly, the
above figures are nowhere near the real numbers given the
social stigma and the high degree of apathy victims encounter.
Also, the depiction in percentages veils the fact that we are
talking about millions of victims here.

Sometimes it makes me wonder if we have got our understanding of 'terror' all mixed up. The underlying essence of
'terror' is the ability of a small group of individuals to exert
compellence on a much larger majority, forcing the latter to
alter its behaviour. To that extent, rising crime against women
and children is probably the most heinous kind of 'terror' that
India suffers for three reasons. First, it is perpetrated by fellow

citizens and not some sinister external force. As a matter of fact, in the majority of rape and sexual abuse cases, the victim knows and at times is related to the perpetrators. Second, the trauma of the victims continues far beyond the incident itself as they are scarred for life—physically, psychologically, and socially. But what probably puts this crime in the worst category is the fact that most instances are suppressed, allowing the perpetrators the impunity to strike again and again.

Like all crimes, our society pays a price for this at several levels. Studies show that survivors of such traumatic events continue to be dysfunctional and often become pathological committers themselves. Abused children have much higher proclivity towards violence and crime and most rape victims are suboptimal for the rest of their lives.

Without absolving law-enforcement authorities, or condoning their insensitivity at times, society at large is equally responsible for rape, sexual abuse, and domestic violence. The latter atrocity clearly shows that the answer does not lie in just better policing or deploying more uniforms around the city. Instead, society, its exemplars and every individual are in some sense accountable for the deterioration.

While rape, sexual abuse, and domestic violence are clearly three different crimes, their common thread is low rates of reporting. Estimates suggest that over 75 percent of rape cases are never reported. Reporting of sexual abuse and domestic violence is even lower. This clearly indicates that the 'pareto' of addressing these crimes lies in creating an environment that fosters disclosure rather than suppression, which only emboldens the perpetrator. And again, while measures such as sensitizing law-enforcement authorities, assigning women police officers or protecting the identity of the victim are important, they still address the smaller percentage of cases where the victims and their families muster enough courage to approach the police. That is because society still treats rape and abuse as 'personal' crimes where the victim has a Hobson's choice of seeking recourse to the law and being subjected to the trauma of a largely apathetic society or just accepting the situation and moving on.

If such crimes have to be addressed forcefully, the answer lies in implementing steps that provide a strong support structure to victims and high deterrence to potential perpetrators. The rape of a woman who works in a mall is an attack on every working woman. Every woman who needs to be out of her house is now forced to be restrained. The abduction and rape of a schoolgirl is an attack on every child that forces each parent to be cautious and constrain their child's childhood. And while being cautious is common sense, it is definitely not the long-term answer.

Social institutions have a responsibility to create an environment where it is the perpetrators who are afraid and not the other way round. Schools and parents must teach children self-defence. Workplaces, corporates, NGOs, and families must 'own' the responsibility of providing financial, moral, and legal support to victims on a continuing basis. Bystanders must realize that the girl they witness being abducted could have been one of their own and, therefore, must get involved. And society must demand pursuance of such cases with the same fervour as it does for outrages such as terror attacks. For, it is farcical to demand zero tolerance for terrorism in a society which is tolerant of such crimes.

— ◆ —

The Strategic Threats Within

Identification of strategic assets and modernization of the Armed Forces have to proceed simultaneously

A fundamental challenge that nations, especially developing ones like ours, constantly face is resource allocation between defence and development. Regardless of the quagmire that our defence modernization process is—it is irrefutable that we expend a large part of our gross domestic product towards defence. Having said that, it is also important to appreciate the strategic shift of threats over the last two decades lest we miss the woods for the trees.

The Indian Armed Forces have historically been organized to defend against external aggression from land and to a lesser extent from coastlines. The bulk of our troop deployment is facing Pakistan, China, Bangladesh, and Myanmar. The former two are obviously considered higher risk for historical reasons. While our conventional forces provide a strong deterrence from inimical neighbours, after 1971, the threat spectrum has shifted from conventional all-out war, to irregular but economically draining battles. Even Kargil, which had overtones of a regular military operation, was a limited 'incursion' rather than an all-out effort to seize any meaningful chunk of territory. 'Set piece' conventional war involves capture or destruction of strategic towns with the aim of forcing the enemy to the negotiating table or degrading them economically.

However, the development of the new instrument of warfare—terrorism, has demoted conventional threats for which our defence forces had been traditionally organized and continue to be funded. The benefit of this instrument is that, while it can be state sponsored and controlled, it has the advantage of deniability and precise deployment. Consider the following scenarios.

Sixty percent of our country's container cargo is handled by just one port location—the Mumbai/Jawaharlal Nehru Port Trust (JNPT). Despite having 7,500 km of coastline, our economic jugular continues to be held in this port which can be struck and put out of action for days if not weeks by a team no larger than those who assaulted Mumbai in 2008. The resulting potential of damage doesn't have to be war-gamed hypothetically. We have empirical evidence from the collision of two ships in August 2010 when the port had to be closed during which over $4 billion worth of cargo was affected. And that was just accident without the accompanying fear psychosis of a terrorist strike.

India has the world's largest oil refinery in Jamnagar. In an eventuality of its take down, India could grind to a halt in a matter of days. While the facility is spread over several hundred acres and well protected, its close proximity to Pakistan and location on the coastline continue to make it a vulnerable point.

Forty-five percent of India's air cargo is handled at Mumbai airport which is hemmed inside just 720 acres (compared with 5,000 acres of Delhi). The airport is surrounded by regular and irregular residential areas over which there can be little control especially in this day and age when shoulder-fired missiles or high explosives are easily available from underground arms markets. Regular thefts from cargo hold areas clearly prove that hostile elements can gain access to them.

The entire airport, including the criss-crossing runway, is in easy line of sight of even a rudimentary shoulder fired missile.

The 26/11 attacks on Mumbai were a paradigm shift in the way terror strikes are maturing. While there have been far more devastating and terrorizing strikes, such as the Beslan School attack in Chechnya or the 9/11 in New York, Mumbai attacks showed the extent of economic damage that 10 men with assault rifles and grenades could achieve. The 'bang for buck' both from an investment and deniability perspective will not be lost on potential terrorists who will focus such attacks on the Achilles heel of the Indian economy—which are its logistics nodes.

The tactical way of addressing these risks would be to strengthen security of such nodal areas, but that has a diminishing point of return or as in the case of JNPT or the Mumbai airport is simply implausible beyond an extent. But if India were to consider addressing such risks strategically, we would soon realize that placing all eggs in one basket is not just suicidal from a security point of view, but is also a suboptimal way of organizing our resources. With the fourth largest coastline in the world, increased investment in port management all along the country is not just good economic sense; it is also solid security strategy. Similarly, relocating cargo terminals away from the proximity of major cities reduces fuel consumption, road congestion, and overall storage costs drastically. Such strategic redesigns would pay for themselves in simply the resultant efficiencies.

It is an old adage that generals continue to fight the previous wars. Our previous wars were highlighted by their focus on territorial gains rather than economic damage. However, if we were to consider the eventual objective of war—it has always been degradation of the adversary's economic prowess. To that extent, while we need to address the modernization of our forces, it is also time we started considering the identification and arraignment of our strategic assets.

— ◈ —

The Age of Mind Wars

Nations must stop fighting today's battles
with yesterday's tools

In warfare, commanders are trained to capture their theatre's 'ground of tactical importance', or GTI. The textbook definition of GTI is that piece of land, the loss of which renders the defender incapable of fighting the battle. In conventional warfare, GTI is usually a dominating height such as Tiger Hill in Kargil or beachheads in Normandy. Failure to control this 'centre of gravity' is a deal breaker, resulting in certain defeat for the side which loses it.

However, in asymmetric warfare, the centre of gravity shifts from physical 'ground' to abstract perceptions. Nations realized this shift when insurgents struck using guerilla-style operations, inflicted damage and disappeared into the hinterland, avoiding head-on battles with security forces. The objective here was not to capture any ground. Instead, it was to show the local populace that they were more powerful than the government. In this context, the centre of gravity became the support of local villagers wooed both by insurgents and security forces—the former portraying themselves as 'freedom fighters' and the latter representing the law.

Though it took some time for conventional forces to recognize this changing paradigm, the doctrine of 'winning hearts and minds' evolved as a necessary weapon to counter insurgency. The change was not easy as most senior commanders were from the old school whose focus was on use of force, intelligence, and tools of law enforcement. Leveraging non-kinetic operations such as information warfare or projection of soft power was scoffed upon as 'unsoldier-like'.

However, this aspect exacerbated in the context of terrorism because here the centre of gravity is perception of key public audiences who are not limited to any geographical location. The metric that has most meaning for terrorists is not the number of people killed or the value of property destroyed. Instead, it is the amount of attention they draw to their attack— and consequently to their identity and ideology. Or in other words, the effectiveness with which terrorists communicate their ideology and strategy to capture public perception, which in the media age means rapid information dissemination.

Until recently, governments could afford to ignore this because they controlled the media which was surrogate of influencing, if not outright controlling, perception. But three tools of the digital revolution changed that dramatically. These were the digital camera, easy-to-use editing software and the new tools of Internet. Unsurprisingly, terrorists groups were quick to recognize the potential of this novel instrument of war. As counter-insurgency expert Thomas Hammes points out—insurgent strategy shifted from military campaigns supported by information operations—to strategic communication campaigns supported by terrorist operations. There are several reasons why communication campaigns have become the centre of gravity with terrorist acts supporting them, rather than the other way round.

The first is fundamental to all conflicts—propagation of an alternative ideology. An ideology does not have to be based on truth to be believed. It just has to be communicated effectively and persuasively in a favourable cultural, socio-economic, and political environment. Persecution of minorities, ethnic cleansing, communal and religious conflicts, etc., all leverage this essential principle. The tools of Web 2.0 such as social networking platforms, YouTube, and blogs allow powerful and unfettered advocacy of ideology. As early as 2005, key Al

Qaeda leaders instructed their cohorts to capture the hearts and minds of the masses and commended the 'mujahideen of the information front line' recognizing that their efforts—sound, video, and text—were more lethal than rockets and missiles. In July 2007, *The Economist* noted that the handheld video camera had become as important a tool for insurgency as the AK-47. The terrorist communication process has now evolved to a point where they control the entire production and distribution and can target multiple audiences with precise messaging in multiple languages.

The second reason is that terrorists can use the Web 2.0 with complete impunity and safety. In September 2004, a terrorist group in Iraq beheaded three Western hostages and posted the video on websites and blogs. In a chilling sequel in January 2007, a similar plot to kidnap and behead a hostage live on a webcast was disrupted in the UK. As Aidan Winn of Kings College points out, the nature of this plot was very different from previous attacks causing mass casualties. It is believed that as improved security measures and better intelligence thwart large-scale attacks, terrorists will resort to macabre acts such as beheadings and leverage their publicity as the new weapon of terror.

Terrorist organizations have elevated their communication strategy beyond one-way information. In 2008, Ayman al-Zawahiri responded to several hundred questions posted by the public in a video. The Web allowed a terrorist leader on the run—to interact with millions of his target audience.

Marshall McLuhan's famous aphorism 'the medium is the message' is reinforced in the current scenario where the centre of gravity is rapidly shifting from physical space into the minds of stakeholders. The response of nation states trying to ban dissemination of such content is ineffectual and counterproductive. Democracies have particular challenges in developing counterterrorist strategies without seeming draconian themselves. However, as James Forest, former faculty at the US Military Academy advocates, an approach could be to develop strategies that highlight the inherent contradictions, hypocrisies and internal divisions of terrorist groups and help terrorists defeat themselves rather than trying to defeat them. But to do that, we must stop trying to solve today's problems with yesterday's tools.

Strategic Security by Design

Enhancement of the national security posture makes focus on improving economic security a prerequisite

Nations have the choice to respond to threats with a short-term tactical or a long-term strategic perspective. Of course, these aren't mutually exclusive and a sound approach lies in an optimal mix. However, developing countries such as ours need resources far more in areas of energy, food and water security and despite best intentions, conventional external and internal security often take a back seat. While tactically we can and must implement specific security projects, our strategic thinking cannot be limited to holding two ministries accountable for India's external and internal security.

A nation's need for security is not just confined to its territorial sovereignty. Matter of fact, most flashpoints of conflicts such as the blockade of the Suez Canal or overproduction of oil by Kuwait had nothing to do with territorial conflicts. The US retains its world dominance more by holding sway over the trade routes on the high seas, than it does by stationing troops overseas. Economic sovereignty is as important to national security as territorial sovereignty.

By the same analogy, enhancement of the national security posture pre-requisites a focus on improving economic security. Developing nations, therefore, must use building blocks of economic security in a manner that also improves national security, reducing the need to embark on separate standalone, resource-consuming initiatives. Here are some examples of such opportunities.

Since its announcement in 2006, the unified goods and services tax (GST) has missed two deadlines due to reasons beyond the scope of this discussion. In short, GST envisages doing away with multiple levels of taxation to leverage efficiencies in logistics and investments in warehousing and allied infrastructure. The introduction of GST has such powerful potential that it can add a percentage point to India's gross domestic product!

However, apart from its obvious financial benefits, GST will bring a single unified national goods tracking system, giving visibility of consignments, allowing security officials to better discern outlier behaviour such as movement of narcotics, contraband, human trafficking, and a wide array of illegal activities that is possible today—because of the fragmented nature of logistics in India. GST will reduce waiting time for trucks at state border checkposts, thus diminishing opportunities for pilferage, sabotage, adulteration, and corruption. Security agencies will have the ability to speedily track down the origin and routing of equipment such as mobile phones, computers, or explosives used in illegal activities by querying GST. Trucks can be 'sealed' at the point of origin with no need to open and examine the contents (from a tax perspective) at each transit point. All of this will also free up vast infrastructure that is currently necessary to monitor piecemeal taxation—and focus it on security.

GST will also aid during natural disasters and crises by allowing the free and unrestricted movement of essential equipment, food, and transportation to locations in dire straits. In the past, trucks have waited for hours at checkposts while people were in desperate need of food, water, and medical supplies just a few kilometres away.

Another example is India's pressing requirement of maritime security. The 26/11 Mumbai attacks highlighted the need to secure and monitor the coast, but massive resources are required to guard the 7,000 km-long zone. However, there is a way to hitch a ride on the back of the reforms in maritime policies. Coastal security will improve dramatically because of the sheer increase in maritime traffic along the coast if the reforms are implemented. Paradoxically, despite a multitude of advantages, maritime transportation has remained a neglected area in India. Only 7 percent of cargo in India is carried on marine routes compared with 16 percent in the US and 46 percent in the European Union. Despite the fact that maritime transportation is six times cheaper, has a far smaller carbon footprint, and the ancillary benefits of reducing congestion, pollution and road fatalities, investments in coastal shipping infrastructure is less than a fraction of the spending on roads, rail, and airports.

Like GST, development of maritime corridors will have several collateral benefits for coastal security. For one, escalation in traffic along the coast will defray the cost of patrolling and monitoring the zone. With an increased number of vessels plying along the coast, surveillance, early warning and quick response to emergencies will be much easier as commercial ships are equipped with state-of-the-art radar and communications equipment that security forces will be able to piggyback on, to transmit and receive alerts and advisories. The maritime corridors will also result in the proliferation of ports, jetties and other infrastructure along the coast, creating a lattice of ancillary vessels, establishing a stronger coastal defence system. As coastal economies improve, there will be better communications along the shoreline, which will make it easier to detect and track hostile vessels and reduce the chances of infiltration and smuggling.

In a complex world, security threats themselves are often manifestations of deep festering and interconnected issues. While security forces can be tasked to confront the manifestations and establish an environment of immediate control— strategic thinking lies in leveraging all nation-building projects to create an interlace of security grids that work in symbiotic conjunction. But to do that, we must look beyond parochial interests and heed the words of Benjamin Franklin—that we must indeed all hang together or assuredly we shall all hang separately.

— ◆ —

Breaking the Gridlock

It is high time our generation stops lamenting and starts addressing India's multifaceted challenges

In his book *The Death of Common Sense*, Philip Howard narrates an incident when nuns from Mother Teresa's charity were seeking abandoned buildings owned by New York City. Under the arrangement between Mother Teresa and mayor Ed Koch, the city would hand over the building for a dollar and the charity would refurbish it for the homeless. Providence seemed to smile on the nuns when they found a fire-gutted building that suited their purpose perfectly—until, of course, bureaucracy and law kicked in. After two years of presenting their case to various committees for the transfer of property, the nuns were finally told that as per the rules, they could not commission the building without a lift—notwithstanding the fact that homeless people didn't really care about a lift. Mother Teresa gave up. Though Howard focuses on how the letter of the rule is stifling its intent, the story is familiar in the current Indian context where every system seems to be breaking down under overload, scrutiny, and hindsight ascribing sinister motive to almost every decision.

Whether or not we are indeed going through traumatic times and if we are, then the extent of that trauma, is not really the issue. The point is, it is we—the citizens—who make up the establishments and institutions of the country, and, therefore, it is we who have to fix the situation. And that can't happen in an environment of vitriolic rhetoric, accusations, and distrust. Bad situations cannot be improved by introducing more rules. Instead, existing rules need to be implemented with visionary responsibility. But these days teachers don't comfort children fearing accusations of inappropriate physical contact. Doctors don't treat accident victims fearing embroilment in legalities. Bureaucrats hesitate to take decisive steps fearing accusations of vested interests. Citizens don't trust the police, the media or public institutions and bystanders choose to stand by, instead of pitching in.

One of the most effective weapons of war is the use of psychological operations where the attack is on the will of the nation. Terrorism is a psychological operation that aims to demolish the resolve of a society. But it looks like terrorists needn't bother as we are doing a pretty good job of it ourselves.

India faces multifaceted problems and there is no simple, short-term answer that will satisfy all stakeholders. As a matter of fact, every long-term, sustainable solution comes with short- to medium-term trauma. The answer, however, lies in recognizing some terms of reference within which such solutions will have to be developed.

First of these is a recognition that we must choose our battles carefully. India faces daunting challenges ranging from poverty, unemployment, shortages of water, living space, environmental degradation, illiteracy, corruption and administrative inefficiencies to external and internal security. Crusaders against each problem believe that theirs must get priority, but there has to be some start point and sufficient focus and elbow room given on that to deliver meaningful results.

Most cocktail discussions or policy debates follow a familiar train of conversation. Say corruption is the start point, but that is invariably linked to a multitude of other issues such as election reforms, decision paralysis, illiteracy, vote bank politics, etc. So the net takeaway seems to be that nothing can be resolved until somehow—magically—everything is. But that is neither going to happen and nor is it necessary.

Sometimes to solve problems of the present, we need to look at our past. In his recent book *Accidental India*, Shankkar Aiyar chronicles several catastrophes from whose brink India managed to reassert itself. From a nation that had to physically pledge its gold to one that has several billion dollars in foreign reserves. From a nation that had to live 'ship to mouth' to one that is largely self-sufficient for food, from a nation that had to wait in line for years for a phone connection to one that has a mobile in every pocket. We have been there, and we can do it again.

However to achieve this, we must acknowledge the gravity of situation we are in now and the need to do something about it. But intellectual India seems to be adrift between a sense of hubris and abject despondency. Cynicism and scepticism are self-propagating and self-fulfilling and have the potential to slide an entire populace into depression. The favourite national pastime these days seems to be bemoaning our establishments across the board and herein lies the irony.

Political commentators, leaders, parents and other role models who take great care to shelter their children from bad influences like drugs, alcohol, violence or even abusive language are mindlessly demolishing the edifice of their future. Instead of working towards giving them 'hope of success', they are drumming 'fear of failure' into them. How then do we expect the NextGen to take up the reins of our current problems if our only contribution is to stand by in despairing judgement of the overall situation? Every generation has the onus of improving the environment for their inheritors and it is high time that ours stopped the lamenting and started the fixing.

— ◈ —

Clear and Looming Danger

As we bid farewell to the year that saw closure to a chapter of the 26/11 attacks, it is time to take stock of security challenges that daunt us in the years ahead. The absence of any major security incident in the recent past should not lull us into believing that we are headed towards safer times. Generals are often accused of fighting the last war and that is why we ought to look at risks of the future.

India, like many parts of the world, is going through a period when threat vectors are shifting so rapidly that our decision makers face the danger of being distracted by the irrelevant. None of the issues at hand are in themselves surprising, which is perhaps where the danger lies. Yet each one of them, or more alarmingly, their combination has the potential to be cataclysmic.

Take for instance something as basic as water. According to the Union ministry of water resources, in the next decade eleven major basins will be water deficient. Over half of India's class two towns already subsist on severely limited quantities of water. Over a million tankers are needed to keep these towns supplied. Even water that is available is heavily contaminated exposing over 60 million people to fluoride and arsenic poisoning. It is not that India does not get enough water. It manages to use just half of its accessible precipitation, wasting the rest. Our capability to store water on a per capita basis is a mere 190 cubic meters, which is less than one tenth of China and one thirtieth of the US. Notwithstanding myriad ministries, schemes and plans (or perhaps because of them), India is heading towards a water disaster.

Then, consider food security. Even 50 years after the advent of the green revolution, India ranks below Nigeria and Sudan in its struggle to combat hunger. We are second (behind Bangladesh) in terms of malnourished children in the world and lose four children every minute below the age of five due to largely preventable diseases. Thousand children a day are lost due to diarrhea alone. According to the Global Hunger Index, India is amongst the three countries where the hunger situation worsened between 1996 and 2011, during which time its neighbours such as Pakistan, Nepal and Bangladesh improved their condition. Even Punjab and Kerala—the wheat and rice baskets of India have a number of undernourished children classified as 'serious'. Tellingly, though China began agricultural modernization only in late 1970s, its output per hectare is twice that of India.

Apart from food and water, the atmosphere we live in is graded as one of the worst in the world and ranks 125th in the Environmental Performance Index. India has the third largest number of AIDS infected persons in the world. Further, a recent study pegged the number of those suffering from Hepatitis at more than 40 million. Less than one percent of children are vaccinated for this dreaded disease. All this is happening in a country where healthcare is unaffordable for a vast majority and exorbitantly expensive for the rest.

This list of bewildering dichotomies continues endlessly. A country aspiring to send a mission to Mars has 1.3 million of its citizens scavenging human excreta for a living. Maharashtra—home to one of the wealthiest cities in the world—has the dubious distinction of the highest number of farmer suicides in the country. India ranks fourth in the world in terms of dollar billionaires; it stands at 134 in the Global Development Index, behind Bhutan and almost all countries in South America. Subsistence labourers are routinely forced to sell their children to repay debts while banks offer unsolicited loans for automobiles and jewellery to the higher income groups. The award winning journalist P. Sainath notes that despite major reforms in the agricultural sector—or indeed because of them—the per capita consumption of food has actually declined over the last several years by almost 20 percent.

India has often been described as a land of stark contradictions. There is the rich India and the poor India; urban India and rural India. But perhaps nothing beats the schizophrenic dissonance between 'ideating' India and 'implementation' India.

They say a frog kept in slow heating water will boil to death because it is unable to perceive the increasing heat. Every strategic problem we face today is of a slow but steadily burning nature. Be it water or food shortages, the spread of Naxalism, destruction of natural resources, deterioration of institutions, growth of corruption, or the greatest threat of them all—the meteoric rise in inequality coupled with a large population of disillusioned, cynical, and underemployed youth—none of the issues can be attributed to a sudden turn of events that took our country by surprise.

Instead, this steady erosion of our fabric occurred while we bickered about the inconsequential. The intellectual in us ideates every problem literally to death while our implementation remains abysmal. It will do us well to heed the words of Frederick the Great, that 'It is pardonable to be defeated—but never to be surprised.'

Empower Women Economically

India must make strategic long-term structural changes to
safeguard women in addition to immediate tactical steps

Several events over the years have 'shaken' the country, but
after a few weeks of crescendo, citizens have to move on. The
Delhi rape case, while it occupies high mindshare now, is likely to meet with the same fate. The reason behind this phenomenon is that average citizens have to revert their attention to
routine existential issues and carry on with their lives. Tactical
steps allow a sense of closure but rarely solve the root cause.
The steps taken by the police in the rape case are laudable but
most address protecting the 'weaker' sex rather than empowering them and removing the 'weaker' tag.

The only meaningful and long term way to empower women
is economic empowerment. Simply put, more wealth needs to
be put into the hands of women by making strategic long term
structural changes in addition to immediate tactical ones.
Studies prove that societies where gender diversity is equitable
are not only safer, but economically vibrant. States with higher
ratio of educated working women fare significantly better in
all parameters.

Women in developing countries like India begin almost
with a triple strike. First, they are denied an equal chance to be
born. Society is gunning for them from the foetus stage. If they
are lucky enough to survive infanticide, girls are undernourished compared with male children. The next disability lies in
the terms of differential treatment when it comes to education
with far more girl drop outs from school than males. And girls
who manage to surmount these barriers next face far more
daunting challenges at the workplace. Ironically while women
constitute a majority in rural and urban labour workforces,
their incomes are substantially lower than men.

This problem is further aggravated in urban and semi-urban work settings. While the number of working women in certain sectors such as banking, teaching etc. are somewhat respectable, several others such as manufacturing have no more than token representation and are almost out of bound for them. Schemes targeting the girl child such as pre and postnatal care, nutrition, scholarships etc. contribute towards creating a 'push', but what is also required is a 'pull' towards systematically creating opportunities for women in the mainstream semi and urban workforce. And this is where the private sector needs to be coopted by both government and society at large. Here are some ways to achieve this.

Depending on the sector, private firms must be incentivized for achieving improved gender representation within defined periods. This could be in the form of tax reductions or reduced interest loans for companies that show measurable increased opportunities for women. Efforts such as child care centres at work place, some flexibility in working hours, opportunities to work from home, etc. will add lakhs of women to the workforce literally overnight, as these factors currently keep them away.

Companies can create product branding that shows consumers that they are being produced by a women workforce. Such 'certified' labeling will enable buyers make a conscious choice in supporting these ventures as well as accelerating gender equity in competing organizations.

Conscientious organizations should take the lead in including measures of gender equity into their bottom line reporting as well as their corporate social responsibility measures—not as largesse but with a realization that such steps make strategic business sense in the long run. In turn, investors must reward such steps by supporting such companies.

Unfortunately, the current mindset works in the opposite direction. After every instance of rape or molestation, the typical response is to ban women from being employed after a certain hour or to provide them with escorted home drops. Such measures though well-meaning and even necessary in certain cases, essentially drive up the cost of employing women, and are thus counterproductive in the long run.

At an individual level, consumers don't realize that they in effect incur an economic cost for every such incident. Here is how that happens. In an ideal business environment, students living and getting educated in tier three or four towns 'export' their employability into tier one cities. This way they earn several multiples of the cost of their education and upbringing which is lower in tier three/four cities. But when such instances hit the national narrative, parents from tier three cities are reluctant to send their children into what they rightfully perceive as a dangerous environment thus removing the value chain that 'produces' talent at a lower cost and engages them at higher. The resultant higher cost of talent in tier one cities coupled with incidental costs of provisioning them with secure transportation etc, is eventually borne by the end consumer.

While safeguarding 50 percent of our citizens is undoubtedly a national, social and individual responsibility, the only meaningful and sustainable way of removing the tag of the weaker sex is to empower women economically. And unless the case is advocated from a business perspective—which is rightfully meritorious, every measure will be viewed as a sop or a cost addition. And that is just systematic debilitation, in the guise of empowerment.

— ◆ —

Indifference to Crimes
Against Women

India's leaders are yet to wake up to the upsurge of
public anger on horrific crimes of the kind seen recently

On 13 March, 1964, 29-year-old Kitty Genovese was returning home late night in New York City. As she approached her
house, she noticed a man stalking her and tried to run into
her apartment. The assailant, Winston Moseley, quickly over-
took Kitty and stabbed her twice in the back. Her screams for
help were heard by many neighbours but only one of them,
Robert Moser, bothered to open his window and shout at the
assailant to leave the girl alone. Startled by the shout, Winston
ran away and Kitty, who was seriously injured, dragged herself
into the building where she lay—still unattended. Winston
returned after 10 minutes and, based on his own testimony,
hunted down Kitty, repeatedly stabbed her, raped her while
she was dying and drove away after stealing $49. One of the
dozens of witnesses finally got someone else to call the police,
who arrived too late.

Two weeks later, Martin Gansberg of *New York Times*
published an article in which he accused 38 neighbours and
witnesses of watching a woman being stabbed to death, but not
calling the police—much less trying to intervene. Though the
story was controversial and to some extent inaccurate, the incident triggered research by social psychologists John Darley and
Bibb Latane that showed that contrary to expectations, a larger number of bystanders actually lowered the chances of someone intervening. The reasons for this contrarian behaviour
ranged from people not wanting to get involved (the New York
police department was notoriously hostile to people reporting crimes those days) to feeling uncertain about intervening

when no one else was. Psychologists termed this phenomenon the 'Genovese effect' or 'diffusion of responsibility'.

Notwithstanding the several heinous sexual crimes that have occurred in India—and indeed continue to, even after the one that shook the country, the particular incident of 16 December, 2012 is a paradigm shift for several reasons. First, the angst of the people, especially the youth, has come to a boil where even the gates of Rashtrapati Bhavan were rattled in rage. There is seething anger on the streets and cities of India and while it is being vented on the men in khaki, they are just visible manifestations of our state apparatuses—on whom it is really aimed.

Second, I don't think there is still a recognition that a large part of the anger stems from the perception that no matter what, 'nothing happens.' This sense of 'nothing happens' is not just limited to punishing the guilty. It is a pervasive feeling across the board. A country that was on an aggressive growth path with first world aspirations is hobbled by processes, procedures, maladies, and mindsets that haven't changed fast enough.

Third, it would be naïve to assume that making some laws more stringent will make this angst go away. This anguish is not about the leniency of the laws, it is about the inability of the establishment that is supposed to create and uphold the entire value chain of a lawful, economically vibrant, clean, and wholesome society. The police are just the last mile symbol of it and therefore get more than their share of the brickbats.

Finally, it is also time that each of us introspect why we don't get involved. If any of us was in a car right behind that bus, and caught a glimpse of a girl screaming for help, how many of us would decide to give chase or at the very least dial the police. Before answering that question, it might be better to recollect how often have we got involved when we witnessed an injured man lying on the road after an accident or even stopped our vehicle to help a blind person cross the road. For that matter, even in the Delhi incident, the two mangled victims lay on the road with people gawking but not stepping forward to help.

Certainly, some of us don't get involved because we fear subsequent harassment by the police—and we must fight to change such abject wrongdoings.

But many of us also don't get involved because we believe someone else will be doing something about it, thus diffusing our own responsibility. We have to change that too.

When Kitty's murderer was finally caught, he confessed to not only having killed her but two other women as well. Though Winston was incarcerated for life and denied parole 14 times, he managed to escape once, grievously maim people, and commit yet another rape before being recaptured after a two-day manhunt. But the punishment of Winston Moseley or the apathy of the New York Police does not absolve the witnesses who saw Kitty being murdered and did nothing. Winston, 78 now, is still serving time in jail whereas the neighbours who could have intervened, but didn't, walked away scot-free.

It would be a pity if we sought closure of this incident by just punishing six perpetrators instead of realizing our responsibility of changing the sub-optimal environment we have come to accept as fait accompli.

The Rape of our Children

The primal anger such crimes evoke and the subsequent baying for blood is hypocritical escapism from the reality that every member of society is accountable for the overall behaviour of that society

The current violence against children in India begets an introspective question. Is this a new phenomenon, or have such cruelties always been happening and we are just more aware of them now? Unfortunately, the latter is probably closer to the truth. It is, of course, convenient to label these instances as the ghastly handiwork of deranged perverts, call for drawing and quartering them to achieve closure and move on. But the primal anger such crimes evoke and the subsequent baying for blood—anybody's blood—is hypocritical escapism from the reality that every member of society is accountable for the overall behaviour of that society.

For a moment, let's step back from the sexual act of rape and consider how our society treats the helpless in general and children in particular.

It is a pathetic paradox that millions of children live on the streets of a country that has aspirations of achieving superpower status. Children, many of them infants, forage in garbage bins, use cardboard as shelter, eat putrid food, get stoned and beaten frequently. Children who manage to survive infant mortality, fatal diseases, accidents, abandonment and other life-threatening abuses live in packs under bridges, deserted buildings, pavements and railway stations. Children as young as 5 are put to work as rag pickers, beggars, foragers, and prostitutes. They get no vaccination against basic diseases, no medical assistance whatsoever, and have no one they can ask for help. Simple cuts fester into gangrene and fractures into pain-

ful and torturous deformities. In addition, they are beaten, hit
by vehicles, raped, sodomized, separated from siblings, sold
and at times killed. All of this happens literally a stone's throw
away from where we live. Even considering the ridiculous fraction of recorded versus actual statistics, as per the National
Crime Records Bureau figures, more than 5,000 children are
raped and over 1,000 killed each year. There are, of course, a
plethora of laws to protect children, but they don't seem to
make a difference.

Child labour is our wretched euphemism for child slavery and
our country holds the dubious distinction of having the highest
number of child workers in the world. Children are employed
in occupations ranging from back-breaking work as labourers
and handling hazardous chemicals to manual scavenging and
sexual gratification. Even the suppressed figure of 60 million
child workers heralds the shame of our nation and apathy
of its people. Again there is no dearth of laws banning child
labour, manual scavenging, or child trafficking for that matter.

Such examples of systemic abuse can go on, but the crux is
that as a society, we are inured to exploitation of the helpless,
poor and especially the voiceless. A sporadic outburst in the
aftermath of one instance may act as a pressure release for the
frustrated society, but it doesn't make any meaningful difference. After the customary time span in air and print, the issue
is pushed into the background by yet another round of scams
and contemporary 'breaking news'.

The harsh reality is that most of us are fairly tolerant of
exploitation per se. Or at least tolerant of a certain degree of
it. But the problem is that like cancer, there is no mild version
of exploitation. Once a society condones it for convenience,
then mistreatment of the marginalized spirals out of control.

As indeed it has. And while candlelight vigils and rocking the gates of Rashtrapati Bhawan are some ways of expressing angst, it is also time to consider 'direct action' at individual levels.

For instance, in 2010, Sonal, a young MBA working with an advertising firm, witnessed an eight-year-old girl being sent to a brothel by her own poverty-stricken mother in the slums of west Delhi. Within months, Sonal quit her job and started a tiny NGO with just a few thousand rupees. Three years later, her NGO Protsahan (Encouragement) helps over 150 young girls who are 'at risk' by educating and training them for a livelihood. Protsahan has found fledgling benefactors, and surmounted the woes that besiege all noble intentions and even registered into the radar of the World Bank.

Sceptics will scoff—as they always do—at the minuscule difference that any NGO can make in the overall scheme of things, especially when there are millions of children who are at risk out there. But there are also thousands of Sonals and it is the responsibility of any self-respecting society to make it easier for the Sonals of the world to do what each one of us should be doing as well.

This is not just about supporting NGOs though. It is about understanding that meaningful changes don't happen by a surge or demonstration of force alone. They happen by keeping that fervour alive day after day, month after month. Whether it is by imploring conventional media to keep sustained pressure or by applying sustained pressure through social media. Whether it is by seeking out small causes and fighting for them one step at a time, or by actively supporting those who are fighting against systemic apathy.

The father of our nation once said that a country of 350 million people cannot be ruled by 100,000 Englishmen if they refused to cooperate. Sadly a nation of 1.2 billion people cannot be governed by a few hundreds of thousands from the establishment either—if they don't want to be governed well. It is time we realized that nation-building is a contact sport and cannot be played from the sidelines.

Burning Stations and Governance

India is a hard country to administer. Silo mentalities
and turf wars make the task much more difficult

On 18 November, 1987, a major fire broke out at King's Cross
station of the London underground. The start of the fire—a
burning tissue—was seen and reported to Philip Bricknell, a
ticket collector. Bricknell promptly investigated this report
but did not see it through or even mention the incident to
anybody. A separate department handled fire safety and this
ticket collector was simply following the unwritten code of the
underground by not transgressing his remit. At that time, the
underground was operated by the four chief engineers—civil,
signal, electrical, and mechanical—who ran their departments
as fiercely guarded fiefs and jealously protected turfs. Bricknell,
like all other employees, was ingrained with the unwritten rule
of never calling the fire brigade or even mentioning the word
'fire' aloud, lest it cause a stampede. And even if he wanted to,
the strict chain of command forbade Philip from contacting
another department without authorization of his superior.

King's Cross was one of London's oldest stations with much
of the structure still comprising the original material—wood
and rubber. The ceiling of the station had been painted many
times without removing previous layers of highly inflammable
paint. The burning tissue was in fact, part of a much larger
inferno that quickly spread through the station, fuelled by
combustible material.

Eventually Christopher Hayes, the safety inspector of King's
Cross, began investigating the fire but still did not consider
it necessary to involve the fire brigade. Ironically, dozens of
studies by the London fire brigade had chastised the lack of
training and preparedness of the underground staff and their
inadequate knowledge of fire-fighting systems. Just two years

before, the fire brigade had given specific instructions that they be informed at the earliest signs of fire. But Hayes was not aware of this, as the letter had been sent to the operations department. Hayes was not even aware of a sprinkler system that had already been installed to prevent just such an event because that was managed by another division and simply strode past it. Similarly, as in the past, operations had suggested that old paint be removed before fresh coats were applied but the maintenance department had advised them against interfering in their domain.

When the fire brigade finally arrived, they chose to use the fire hydrants installed at the street level and run the hoses all the way down, instead of using those inside the station because their rules forbade operating hydrants of other organizations. As each train pulled into the station, disgorging more passengers, the fire was fuelled further with oxygen. The terrified passengers could not get back into the train because the drivers had explicit orders not to reopen doors once shut— to prevent tardiness.

A year-long investigation found scores of such well-meaning, but disastrous, rules that contributed to one of the worst tragedies of the London underground that claimed 31 lives and injured dozens. Tightly siloed departments spurned external inputs and focused on protecting turf instead of the larger goal—customer safety.

As the *New York Times* reporter Charles Duhigg points out in his book, *The Power of Habit*, organizations evolve unwritten rules to maintain a delicate balance of power that permits them to operate an environment of contradictions. While actions of individuals or departments may originate from good intentions, they often turn into procedures for protecting turf, ignoring damage to overall objectives. This phenomenon is further exacerbated in large and complex environments (such as governments) where overall goals are designed with a philosophy of 'hope for success' but individual accountability is driven by 'fear of failure'. There are important leads in these examples for what India is currently experiencing.

India is unarguably a country of contradictions. Governing a land of such bewildering diversity requires a complex machinery. But rising complexity brings its own problems, and organizational friction is one big one. While critics deplore the plethora of departments, divisions and ministries, at some level, such complexity is inevitable and when multiple and, all too often, contradictory objectives are to be achieved. Almost all challenges India faces are staggering in scale and consequently the solutions, too, require multiple tradeoffs of efficiency, cost, speed, and caution. For instance, jobs have to be created for millions of citizens, something that requires industrialization on a grand scale, but without damaging an already deteriorating environment. Investment has to be made speedily but without compromising prudence. Corruption has to be stemmed using systems that are inefficient, outdated, and corrupt. Justice has to be delivered speedily but without compromising its quality. Even if one assumes that governance mechanisms are not partisan or are selfless—which they are not, the paradoxes between narrow short-term goals and the broader long-term objectives decelerates progress.

The King's Cross fire illustrates how a disjointed ecosystem of departments led to disaster while individuals in each department were doing what they thought was best from their perspective. A similar situation plagues India. Unless we are able to step back and appreciate the multitude of crises that we are already confronted with, our turf loyalty and parochial goals will be our tragedy of errors.

— ◆ —

We Need a Hero to Fix the Mess

There is a sinking feeling that nothing is happening right and the world is deteriorating every day

If our country's newspapers were dashboards for the state of India's security, they would tell a depressing story. Every page presents the mood and state of the nation that seems appallingly despondent. Rapes of children, deaths of the helpless, torture, nepotism, corruption, apathy, crumbling systems, and the general degradation of society is chronicled in graphic detail. There is a sinking feeling that nothing is happening right and our world is deteriorating every day. And, while we berate failings of our institutions, advocate creation of new ones, ask for new laws, demand resignations and set up inquiries, perhaps we need a more radical answer.

We need a hero. A superman or superwoman to get us out this mess. Fortunately, there is someone who fits the bill perfectly. Before I tell you who that is, let me describe a typical day in the life of this superwoman.

When this superwoman goes for her morning walk, she notices rag pickers leaving for work. The rag pickers are often children between 6 and 10 years old, barefoot, filthy, hungry, and scared. The superwoman asks them to follow her home. The children walk cautiously keeping a distance because they have been beaten by guards for entering gated colonies. Once home, the superwoman gives them old newspapers, magazines and other clothes, plastic utensils and trinkets she isn't using any more. This makes the children's day.

Like Clark Kent, our superwoman drives to her regular day job. Before leaving however, she drops in at the aged neighbours' house for a quick hello and to check if they need anything. Sometimes she helps them fix the Wi-Fi in their house or sort out some other errand, but mostly it's just to make sure that they are okay. Her visit is often the highlight of the day for the old couple.

Unlike Batman, this superwoman doesn't drive like a maniac. As a matter of fact, she makes sure that rickshaw pullers carrying loads or cyclists who are edged out by the cars are given right of way. Like all of us, she is beleaguered by street kids at the traffic lights. She doesn't shun or ignore them though. Instead she hands them small biscuit packets which becomes a meal to a malnourished child. When she runs out of the packets, she just smiles and talks to the kids nicely. And that makes their day.

When the superwoman is at work, she finds time to talk to the peons, cleaners, and other low-paid staff of the organization. Surprisingly, she seems to be the rare one who actually knows their names, details of their children, and their problems. Using her superpowers of treating them as individuals with individual problems, she has discovered that many don't get their actual dues. Part of their rightful salary is withheld by contractors or not credited into their provident funds. They don't know how to go about getting basic things like a voter identity card or a bank account. They also don't know what acts and facilities such as the Right to Education or Aadhaar mean for them. The superwoman finds the time to help them with it. Of course, all she needs to do is teach a few of them and the rest learn on their own. That's how she makes their life a bit better.

Since her co-workers figure that she is a superwoman, those needing help come for advice on issues ranging from sexual harassment to learning the ropes within the city. For instance, young girls from the hinterland have no idea how to handle the challenges of a metro. The superwoman helps them find accommodation, vouches for them, connects them to people who can carpool, and teaches them basic survival skills.

When not working, the superwoman has other super tasks. She sometimes does book readings in the school for the blind. They like this so she records the books and hundreds who can't see can now listen to her. Other times she is involved in resident welfare associations where she starts programmes to help tutor the children of household help. Sometimes she tutors them herself. When she is too busy, she gathers these poor children, switches on the TV at her home, and just lets them watch educational channels for a few hours.

Every year, before the winters set in, she collects old clothes and distributes them to orphanages. Her cache of goodies includes used toys, old books, notebooks, diaries, and the list goes on. She knows that the unused trash of one person can be a prized possession for another and all she needs to do is to make that connect happen.

If she hears about ill treatment of servants in the neighbourhood, she gets involved. If she hears that a neighbour is unwell, she steps in. The superwoman has discovered that there are a thousand ways to be super and most are simple to the point of being mundane and yet sheer miracles for those who need it. All she needs to do is get involved. That's it.

You know who the superperson is—or could be. There is indeed no hero in shining armour who is going to come and rescue us. But there is another definition of a hero. A hero is any individual who, when faced with an undesirable situation, employs the means at her disposal to make that situation better.

We need a hero. And if we want to—we all can be one. All it takes is to get involved.

Epilogue

We live in such an interlocked world today that events across the globe can literally shake up our local ecosystems. Similarly, incidents in the Indian subcontinent have the potential to affect the future course of world events. So while a large part of *Everyman's War* is focussed on the Indian subcontinent, the issues in it are intrinsic to many developing and developed countries.

In the years ahead, India will face myriad, interconnected and overwhelming challenges, each of which will have the ability to debilitate the nation.

As I have sought to describe through my book, national security cannot just be the responsibility of a singular set of institutions, departments or even ministries. In fact, the Home and Defence Ministries in India deal with the manifestation of problems whose roots can be traced to other ministries, historical decisions, geopolitical realities and sometimes just global collateral damage. More often than not, our focus on dealing with the manifestation of these issues distracts us from the greater task of implementing the structural changes needed to deal with the underlying causes.

Undoubtedly one of the greatest challenges we face in the country today is to provide for a burgeoning population of aspirational youth—India's vibrant human resource capital which is feted by global economic forecasters and opinion leaders as the future engine of the country's growth story. But many millions will soon enter the work force and find themselves under or unemployed. Our nation's resources, therefore, must be channeled towards growth-oriented strategies. However, this cannot happen in an environment where security, law and order, corruption, and systemic inefficiencies erode the very psyche of the nation and its faith in the leadership and its plans. More so because each of these issues is inexorably linked with other concomitant factors. For instance, unemployment exacerbates the lack of civic order and secessionist tendencies; and yet instability and lawlessness make people wary of establishing businesses that create much-needed opportunities for employment.

There are certainly no silver bullets or straightforward and simple answers. India's scale, diversity, geopolitical, and religious realities disallow any singular, optimal or clear-cut solution. In addition, there are harsh paradoxes that have to be factored into the equation. For instance, among India's most serious regional threats—one is its second largest trading partner and the other has a symbiotic history that cannot be ignored. India wastes tons of food grain because of lack of infrastructure, while millions of its people starve to death. We are a nation that provides bleeding edge Information Technology services to the world and yet several of our governance apparatuses and processes are based on outdated constructs.

Far too many dots remain unconnected, and will stay that way, until such serious strategic issues find their rightful place in the national discussion or decision forums. Nationwide, deliberations about the marginalized are conspicuous by their absence. I believe this is because most of us do not see the connection between the plight of the 'voice-less' and the nation's well-being. However we can no longer afford to ignore the strong symbiotic relationship between these issues and our future progeny. We cannot afford to shelter ourselves and our children from the true face of 'real' India anymore. Raising the walls of our gated colonies is not going to afford us better security beyond a certain point. Neither is just standing by and decrying our political leadership for failing to improve the situation.

I believe solving any major problem warrants three essential steps. The first is recognition of the pervasive status quo and its implications on us as a country, society, and family. The second is to develop solutions that require structural changes and, be prepared to face the economic and social consequences as well as the ardent detractors of those changes. And the third step is to have the moral rigour to pursue the course relentlessly—until the desired changes ensue.

All of this, however, can only happen if the majority of our nation recognises the implications of maintaining status quo in the medium to long term. And to do that, citizens must start educating themselves about the state of our nation's security and their role in it.

Our future threats will come from asymmetric vectors like internal unrest, terrorism, extremism, psychological operations, cyber war, environmental or ecological disasters, and a possible combination of all of them. And these cannot be overcome with one broad swathe of force, as the use of force alone only exacerbates the problem and rarely achieves any meaningful strategic goals.

At times, India is considered to be a soft state, and perhaps there is a perspective there. However being soft does not necessarily mean being weak. Many times, usually after a terrorist attack, 'experts' extol the virtues of 'hard' responses practised by countries like the US and Israel. They forget the price the US had to pay for their kind of war on terror, in terms of economic devastation, global alienation, incalculable human loss, and absolute misery in countries like Iraq and Afghanistan. I am not sure if the US will end up with fewer enemies when their war on terror ends—if it ever does.

The 'experts' also forget that fathers in Israel have to mandatorily carry handguns when they take their children on school picnics. They forget that when a conscripted Israeli soldier finishes his tour of duty, he usually comes to India on vacation. I would rather India be the country that these soldiers come to vacation, than become the one where they come from. India has the opportunity to show the world that we can be measured in our response—and yet be secure.

But for that, we must leverage our resilience, depth, patience, and vast intellectual reserves to address issues that threaten the present and future, and find sustainable solutions. While we should learn and adopt strategies from other countries, our doctrines must emanate from our own DNA, core strengths, cultural philosophies, and ethos. India needs to have the wisdom and courage to replace outdated monolithic imperial apparatuses with modern, nimble and effective ones. We must also recognize that efforts to make structural changes will encounter contrarian motivations and complex parochial interests that are equal to—if not more daunting than the core challenges themselves. And we must have the foresight to realize that time is running out fast for us and our future generations.

This is indeed, every man's war.

About the Author

Photo Credit: Haran Kumar

Raghu Raman has had a unique mix of career experiences beginning with a decade long stint in the Indian Army, during which he saw operations in Punjab, commanded an active post in the Siachen Glacier, followed by a tour of duty in war-torn Angola as a UN peacekeeper. His last stint with the army was as an instructor at the prestigious School of Armoured Warfare, Ahmednagar, teaching leadership and combat tactics to Young Officers who were being readied to lead troops into operations.

In 1998, Raghu Raman joined the Mahindra Group where he led various group companies, including FirstChoice, Mahindra SSG, and the joint venture between BAE and Mahindra, as their CEO. In 2009, he was appointed by the Government of India to create and lead a project initiated after the 26/11 attacks in Mumbai.

Raghu Raman has taught leadership, change management, analytics, strategy, and persuasion and negotiation skills at leading business schools and organizations as visiting faculty and is a member of the Outstanding Speaker Bureau. He is also a columnist for the leading business newspaper—*Mint* and author of several articles in the area of national security, information technology, strategy, and strategic risk management.